Human Resources Management (HRM) and Globalization

Human Resources Management (HRM) and Globalization

Anu Chadha
Lecturer, Department of Commerce,
Government Degree College,
Kathua, Jammu and Kashmir
and
Amrik Singh Sudan
Associate Professor,
Directorate of Distance Education, University of Jammu

New Century Publications
New Delhi, India

NEW CENTURY PUBLICATIONS
4800/24, Bharat Ram Road,
Ansari Road, Daryaganj,
New Delhi - 110 002 (India)

Tel.: 011-2324 7798, 4358 7398, 6539 6605
Fax: 011-4101 7798
E-mail: indiatax@vsnl.com • info@newcenturypublications.com
www.newcenturypublications.com

Editorial office:
LG–7, Aakarshan Bhawan,
4754-57/23, Ansari Road, Daryaganj,
New Delhi – 110 002

Tel.: 011-4356 0919

First Published: **2015**

ISBN: **978-81-7708-404-7**

Published by New Century Publications and printed at Salasar Imaging Systems, New Delhi.

Designs: Patch Creative Unit, New Delhi.

PRINTED IN INDIA

About the Book

Human resources management (HRM) is a dynamic process of bringing people and organizations together so that the goals of each other are met. Since people constitute the most significant resources of any organization, management of human resources becomes critical for the success of an organization.

With the rapid changes in the business scenario in the recent past, organizations are forced to reorient themselves to meet the new challenges. Technological advances, global competition, demographic changes, information revolution and trends towards service society have changed the rules of the game significantly. In such a scenario, organizations with similar set of resources can gain competitive advantage only through effective and efficient management of resources.

In the changing scenario, HRM is no longer an administrative function but a growth-oriented professional function. Human resources managers have to face a number of challenges for managing the modern knowledge-oriented organizations. In the light of these, several new issues have emerged including talent management, outsourcing, performance management, online recruitment, emotional intelligence, team management and impact of information technology and communications.

This book deals with various aspects of HRM in the context of globalization of world economies.

About the Authors

Ms. Anu Chadha is presently Lecturer, Department of Commerce and Management, Government Degree College, Kathua, Jammu and Kashmir. She obtained her M.Com. degree from the University of Jammu in 1995. She has attended and presented papers at a number of national and international conferences/seminars. She has published 36 research papers and articles in academic journals of repute.

Dr. Amrik Singh Sudan is Associate Professor, Directorate of Distance Education, University of Jammu. He secured his M.Com., M.Phil., and Ph.D. degrees from the University of Jammu. He has published 48 research papers in various journals and edited books. He is the recipient of awards and certificates of excellence from India International Friendship Society, and International Institute of Success Awareness, both based in New Delhi.

Contents

Preface

Human beings are the heartbeat of an organization. They are the brain trust and think tanks of future strategies. Intangible assets, like human capital, decide the use of tangible and material resources innovatively to fulfil the objectives of any business entity. Vision sharing with employees with adequate empowerment constitutes an essential element of human resources management (HRM) strategy. A system of fair compensation for performance and provision of a good *work-life balance* and succession planning become important in the context of the *war for talent*, rising salaries and growing levels of attrition, particularly in developing economies like India.

HRM is a dynamic process of bringing people and organizations together so that the goals of each other are met. Since people constitute the most significant resource of any organization, management of human resources becomes critical for the success of the organization.

With the rapid changes in the business scenario in the recent past, organizations are forced to reorient themselves to meet the new challenges. Technological advances, global competition, demographic changes, information revolution and trends towards service society have changed the rules of the game significantly.

In such a scenario, organizations with similar set of resources can gain competitive advantage only through effective and efficient management of resources. Today, human resources management is no more an administrative function but a growth-oriented professional function. Human resources managers have to face a number of challenges for managing the modern knowledge-oriented organizations. In the light of these, several new issues have emerged including talent management, outsourcing, performance management, online recruitment, emotional intelligence, team management and impact of information technology and communications.

The premise that people provide organizations with an important source of sustainable competitive advantage is established. The effective management of human capital as a determinant of organizational performance is thus accepted. Competition, technology, management and the rise of the new economy, has forced organizations to look for innovative strategies to gain the competitive edge. The role of human resource management in organizations has assumed significance in this context and has been evolving dramatically in recent years.

The successful organizations are using human resources as a strategic partner, investing them with far-reaching transformational roles and responsibilities. This activity involves making the function of managing people the most prioritized activity in the organization and integrating all policies and programmes pertaining to human resources within the framework of a company's strategy. Indian organizations are increasingly turning to the HRM techniques to face the emerging challenges posed by liberalization and globalization.

HRM relates to formulation of strategies by business entities concerning selection, training and rewarding of their personnel.

The subject has assumed added significance in the wake of liberalization and globalization trends sweeping across the world. In the face of intense competition unleashed by market-oriented reforms, firms are vying with each other to acquire competitive advantage to prosper in business and in many cases to survive in business. Every possible strategy is being applied to achieve the explicit and implicit objectives of the firm. HRM has emerged as an important ingredient of the policy mix to score points over the existing and potential competitors.

November 2014

Anu Chadha
Amrik Singh Sudan

1

Human Resources Management (HRM) in the Age of Globalization

Resource management is the efficient and effective deployment of an organization's resources when they are needed. Such resources may include financial resources, inventory, human skills, production resources, or information technology (IT). In the realm of project management, processes, techniques and philosophies as to the best approach for allocating resources, have been developed.

1.1 HRM: Meaning and Components

This is the science of allocating human resources among various projects or business units, maximizing the utilization of available personnel resources to achieve business goals; and performing the activities that are necessary in the maintenance of that workforce through identification of staffing requirements, planning and oversight of payroll and benefits, education and professional development, and administering their work-life needs. Efficient and effective deployment of an organization's personnel resources, where and when they are needed, and being in possession of the tools, training and skills required by the work, are pre-requisites of HRM. One such resource management technique is resource levelling, which aims at smoothing the stock of resources on hand thereby reducing both excess inventories and shortages. The required data includes demand for various resources, reasonable forecast by time period into the future, as well as the resources' configurations required in those demands, and the supply of the resources, again forecast by time period into the future as far as possible.

The principle is to invest in resources as stored capabilities and then unleash the capabilities as demanded.

A dimension of resource development is included in resource management by which investment in resources can be retained by a smaller additional investment to develop a new capability that is demanded, at a lower investment than disposing of the current resource and replacing it with another that has the demanded capability.

Human resource management (HRM) is the strategic and coherent approach to the management of an organisation's most valued assets—the people working there who individually and collectively contribute to the achievement of the objectives of the business. The term *human resources management* has largely replaced the term *personnel management* as a description of the processes involved in managing people in organizations.

HRM may include:

- Organisational Management.
- Personnel Administration.
- Personnel Management.
- Manpower Management.
- Industrial Management.

However, these traditional expressions are becoming less common for the theoretical discipline. Sometimes even industrial relations and employee relations are confusingly listed as synonyms, although these normally refer to the relationship between management and workers and the behaviour of workers in companies.

The theoretical discipline is based primarily on the assumption that employees are individuals with varying goals and needs, and as such should not be thought of as basic business resources, such as trucks and filing cabinets. The field takes a positive view of workers, assuming that virtually all wish to contribute to the enterprise productively, and that the main obstacles to their endeavours are lack of knowledge, insufficient training, and failures of process.

HRM is seen by practitioners in the field as a more innovative view of workplace management than the traditional approach. Its techniques force the managers of an enterprise to express their goals with specificity so that they can be understood and undertaken by the workforce, and to provide the resources needed for them to successfully accomplish their assignments. As such, HRM techniques, when properly practiced, are expressive of the goals and operating practices of the enterprise overall. HRM is also seen by many to have a key role in risk reduction within organisations.

Synonyms such as personnel management are often used in a more restricted sense to describe activities that are necessary in recruiting the workforce, providing its members with payroll and benefits, and administrating their work-life needs. Hence, if we move to actual definitions, Torrington and Hall (1987) define personnel management as, "being a series of activities which, first enables working people and their employing organisations to agree about the objectives and nature of their working relationship and, secondly, ensures that the agreement is fulfilled".

While Miller (1987) suggests that HRM relates to, "those decisions and actions which concern the management of employees at all levels in the business and which are related to the implementation of strategies directed towards creating and sustaining competitive advantage".

1.2 Academic Theory of HRM

The goal of human resource management is to help an organization to meet strategic goals by attracting, and maintaining employees and also to manage them effectively. The key word here perhaps is "fit", i.e. a HRM approach seeks to ensure a fit between the management of an organization's employees, and the overall strategic direction of the company (Miller, 1989).

The basic premise of the academic theory of HRM is that humans are not machines, therefore we need to have an interdisciplinary examination of people at the workplace. Fields such as psychology, industrial engineering, legal/paralegal studies and organizational psychology, industrial relations, sociology, and critical theories like post-modernism and post-structuralism, play a major role.

One widely used scheme to describe the role of HRM, developed by Dave Ulrich, defines 4 fields for the HRM function: (a) strategic business partner, (b) change agent, (c) employee champion, and (d) administration.

However, many HR functions these days struggle to get beyond the roles of administration and employee concerns, and are seen rather as reactive, than being proactive partners for the top management.

In addition, HR organizations also have the difficulty in proving how their activities and processes add value to the company. Only in the recent years, HR scholars and HR professionals are focusing to develop models that can measure, if HR adds value.

1.3 Critical Academic Theory

Post-modernism plays an important part in academic theory and particularly in critical theory. Indeed, Karen Legge in "Human Resource Management: Rhetorics and Realities", poses the debate of whether HRM is a modernist project or a post-modern discourse (Legge, 2004).

In many ways, critically or not, many writers contend that HRM itself is an attempt to move away from the modernist traditions of personnel (man as machine) towards a post-modernist view of HRM (man as individuals).

Critiques include the notion that because 'human' is the subject we should recognize and that people are complex and that it is only through various discourses that we can understand the world.

Critical theory also questions whether HRM is the pursuit of "attitudinal shaping", particularly when considering empowerment, or perhaps more precisely pseudo-empowerment, as the critical perspective notes. Many critics note that the move away from 'man as machine', is often in many ways, more a linguistic (discursive) move away than a real attempt to recognise the human in human resource management.

Critical theory, in particular post-modernism (post-structualism), recognises that because the subject is people in the workplace, the subject is a complex one, and therefore simplistic notions of 'the best way' or unitary perspectives on the subject are too simplistic. It also considers the complex subject of power, power games and office politics. Power in the workplace is a vast and complex subject that cannot be easily defined. This leaves many critics to suggest that management 'gurus', consultants, best practice and HR models are often overly simplistic, but in order to sell an idea, they are simplified, and often lead management as a whole to fall into the trap of oversimplifying the relationship.

1.4 HRM Processes

Human resources management comprises several processes. Together they are supposed to achieve the above mentioned goal. These processes can be performed in an HR department, but some tasks can also be outsourced or performed by line-managers or other departments.

- Workforce planning.
- Recruitment.
- Induction and orientation.
- Skills management.
- Training and development.
- Personnel administration.
- Compensation in wage or salary.
- Time management.
- Travel management (sometimes assigned to accounting rather than HRM).
- Payroll (sometimes assigned to accounting rather than HRM).
- Employee benefits administration.
- Personnel cost planning.

- Performance appraisal.

1.5 Careers in HRM

The sort of careers available in HRM are varied. There are generalist HRM jobs such as human resource assistant. There are careers involved with employment, recruitment and placement and these are usually conducted by interviewers, EEO (equal employment opportunity) specialists or college recruiters. Training and development specialism is often conducted by trainers and orientation specialists. Compensation and benefits tasks are handled by compensation analysts, salary administrators, and benefits administrators.

Professional organizations in HRM include the Society for Human Resource Management, the Australian Human Resources Institute (AHRI), the Chartered Institute of Personnel and Development (CIPD), the International Public Management Association for HR (IPMAHR), Management Association of Nepal (MAN) and the International Personnel Management Association of Canada (IPMA-Canada).

1.6 Difference between Personnel Management and HRM

In conservation, resource management is a set of practices pertaining to maintaining natural system integrity. Examples of this form of management are air resource management, soil conservation, forestry, wildlife management and water resource management. The broad term for this type of resource management is natural resource management (NRM).

Some experts assert that there is no difference between human resources and personnel management. They state that the two terms can be used interchangeably, with no difference in meaning. In fact, the terms are often used interchangeably in help-wanted ads and job descriptions.

For those who recognize a difference between personnel management and human resources, the difference can be described as philosophical. Personnel management is more administrative in nature, dealing with payroll, complying with employment law, and handling related tasks. Human resources, on the other hand, is responsible for managing a workforce as one of the primary resources that contributes to the success of an organization.

When a difference between personnel management and human resources is recognized, human resources is described as much broader in scope than personnel management. Human resources is said to incorporate and develop personnel management tasks, while seeking to create and develop teams of workers for the benefit of an organization. A primary goal of human resources is to enable employees to work to a maximum level of efficiency.

Personnel management can include administrative tasks that are both traditional and routine. It can be described as reactive, providing a response to demands and concerns as they are presented. By contrast, human resources involve ongoing strategies to manage and develop an organization's workforce. It is proactive, as it involves the continuous development of functions and policies for the purposes of improving a company's workforce.

Personnel management is often considered as an independent function of an organization. Human resource management, on the other hand, tends to be an integral part of overall company function. Personnel management is typically the sole responsibility of an organization's personnel department. With human resources, all of an organization's managers are often involved in some manner, and the chief goal may be to have managers of various departments develop the skills necessary to handle personnel-related tasks.

As far as motivators are concerned, personnel management typically seeks to motivate employees with such things as compensation, bonuses, rewards, and the simplification of work responsibilities. From the personnel management point of view, employee satisfaction provides the motivation necessary to improve job performance. The opposite is true of human resources. Human resource management holds that improved performance leads to employee satisfaction. With human resources, work groups, effective strategies for meeting challenges, and job creativity are seen as the primary motivators. When looking for a job in personnel management or human resources, it is important to realize that many companies use the terms interchangeably. If you are offered a job as a personnel manager, you may be required to perform the same duties as a human resource manager, and vice versa. In some companies, a distinction is made, but the difference is very subtle.

1.7 Globalisation: Features and Dimensions

Globalisation implies widening and deepening integration with the globe, i.e. with people and processes abroad. The trend towards the evolution of a global society is generally thought of in economic terms and in terms of the consequences of the revolution in communication technologies. There is undoubtedly much greater economic integration among the nations of the world today. Globalisation is widely seen as the most important factor that could influence economies of nations the world over in the new millennium. The rapid advancement in information technology and communications has made it not just possible but absolutely essential for economies of the world to adapt or fall by the wayside.

The 1990s witnessed a paradigm shift towards market-oriented economic policies and a careful dismantling of obstacles in its wake. This has helped the smaller, emerging economies gain access to world markets, emergent technologies and collaborations. This has also given them a window to the developed world and helped them understand the significant role of globalisation as an instrument, which could be utilised not just to achieve economic efficiency, but also eradicate poverty.

Globalisation has also resulted in the creation of a new business framework. More changes can be expected in the business scenario specifically in terms of openness, adaptiveness and responsiveness. The most important dimensions of economic globalisation are: (a) breaking down of national barriers; (b) international spread of trade, financial and production activities, and (c) growing power of transnational corporations and international financial institutions in these processes. While economic globalisation is a very uneven process, with increased trade and investment being focused in a few countries, almost all countries are greatly affected by this process.

A major feature of globalisation is the growing concentration and monopolisation of economic resources and power by transnational corporations and by global financial firms and funds. This process has been termed transnationalisation, in which fewer and fewer transnational corporations are gaining a large and rapidly increasing proportion of world economic resources, production and market shares. Where a multinational company used to dominate the market of a single product, a big transnational company (TNC) now typically produces or trades in an increasing multitude of products, services and sectors. Through mergers and acquisitions, fewer and fewer of these TNCs now control a larger and larger share of the global market, whether in commodities, manufactures or services.

Another feature of the current globalisation process is the globalisation of national policies and policy-making mechanism. National policies (including economic, social, cultural and technological) that until recently were determined by the States and people within a country have increasingly come under the influence of international agencies and processes or by big private corporations and economic/financial players. This has led to the narrowed ability of governments and people to make choices from options in economic, social and cultural policies.

Most developing countries have seen their independent policy-making mechanism capacity eroded, and have to adopt policies influenced by other entities, which may on balance be detrimental to the countries concerned. The developed countries, where the major economic players reside, and which also control the processes and policies of international economic agencies, are better able to maintain control over their own national policies as well as determine the policies and practices of international institutions and the global system. However, it is also true that the large corporations have taken over a large part of decision-making even in the developed countries, at the expense of the power of the state or political and social leaders.

1.8 Globalisation and Developing Countries

The issue that concerns developing countries is how one can ensure greater participation of the weaker economies in the global process and what needs to be done to ensure that the course of globalisation benefits more people in more countries. The uneven and unequal nature of the present globalisation is manifested in the fast growing gap between the rich and poor people of the world and between developed and developing countries; and by the large differences among nations in the distribution of gains and losses.

This imbalance leads to polarisation between countries and groups that gain, and the many countries and groups in society that lose out or are marginalised. Globalisation, polarisation, wealth concentration and marginalisation are therefore linked through the same process. In this process, investment resources, growth and modern technology are focused on a few countries, mainly in North America, Europe, Japan and a few East Asian countries. A majority of developing countries are excluded from the process, or are participating in it in marginal ways.

Although the developed world is in a dominant position and has been prepared to use this to further their control of the global economy, the developing countries have not done well in organising themselves to co-ordinate on substantial policy and negotiating positions. The developed countries, on the other hand, are well-organised within their own countries, with well-staffed departments dealing with international trade and finance, and with university academics and private and quasi government think tanks helping to obtain information and map policies and strategies. They also have well-organised associations and lobbies associated with their corporations and financial institutions, which have great influence over the government departments.

On the positive side, globalisation has compelled developing countries to improve overall economic management, and make their economies efficient. To get a share of global capital and technology, developing countries have to upgrade their social and economic institutions through administrative, legislative and legal reforms. The quality of governance has to improve to encourage productivity and efficiency. Political stability has to be established. In this context, following lessons can be drawn from the East Asian countries:

1. Developing human capital is a basic pre-requisite. Successful globalisation and a knowledge economy require educated, healthy and skilled people.
2. It is necessary to build up domestic savings and put them to productive use.
3. Sound economic management and macroeconomic balances are necessary. Large fiscal deficit is a serious obstacle to globalisation.
4. Good governance at the national and sub-national levels builds confidence among investors.
5. Transparency has to be established in the functioning of both government and business units.
6. Free and open market economies require effective regulatory authorities because role of government changes from control and regulation to governance and facilitation.
7. Modernised capital markets with effective regulatory authorities are necessary to impart confidence to investors by maintaining stability and regulating speculative forces.

1.9 Opportunities Offered by Globalization

Science and technology, as fundamental components of development, are transforming patterns of production, contributing to the creation of jobs and new job classifications, and ways of working, and contributing to the establishment of a knowledge-based society. Technological change can bring new opportunities for all women in all fields if they have equal access, and adequate training. Women should also be actively involved in the definition, design, development, implementation and gender impact evaluation of policies related to these changes. Many women worldwide are yet to effectively use these new communications technologies for networking, advocacy, exchange of information, business, education, media consultation and e-commerce initiatives. For instance, millions of the world's poorest women and men still do not have access to and benefits from science and technologies and are currently excluded from this new field and the opportunities it presents.

The patterns of migratory flows of labour are changing. Women and girls are increasingly involved in internal, regional and international labour migration to pursue many occupations mainly in farm labour, domestic work and some forms of entertainment work. While this situation increases their earning opportunities and self-reliance, it also exposes them—particularly the poor, uneducated, unskilled and/or undocumented migrants—to inadequate working conditions, increased health risk, the risk of trafficking, economic and sexual exploitation, racism, racial discrimination and xenophobia, and other forms of abuse.

Further, globalization has dramatically changed the conditions under which the work for gender equality must be carried out, especially in high growth countries like India. While globalization has generated opportunities for local producers and entrepreneurs to reach international markets, it has at times intensified existing inequalities and insecurities for many poor women. Since the gains of globalization are often concentrated in the hands of those with higher education—those who own resources and have access to capital—poor women are usually the least able to seize the longer term opportunities offered.

This disadvantage has been exacerbated as in most of the countries, policies reflect a commitment to global norms of markets and social policy is increasingly determined by market dynamics. Market friendly policies generate high growth rates that fail to translate into improved standards of health, education and human security. Feminist scholars have highlighted the gendered impact of such policies, many of which increase women's job vulnerability, unpaid work burden, while reducing state level resources that might be used to provide a social safety net. Owing to dissent voiced by feminist scholars on the widespread assumption that gender inequality as a challenge can be overcome with effective and sustained advocacy as it is more about mindsets and less about policies, especially economic policies, there have been some attempts to integrate economic and social policies but gender concerns have not been accorded requisite attention. These disadvantages have led to a situation where gains in women's economic opportunities lag behind those in women's capabilities.

1.10 Globalization of Human Resources

When it comes to business, the world is indeed becoming a smaller place. More and more companies are operating across geographic and cultural boundaries. While most have adapted to the global reality in their operations, many are lagging behind in developing the human resource policies, structures, and services that support globalization.

The human resource function faces many challenges during the globalization process, including creating a global mindset within the HR group, creating practices that will be consistently applied in different locations/offices while also maintaining the various local cultures and practices, and communicating a consistent corporate culture across the entire organization.

To meet these challenges, organizations need to consider the HR function not as just an administrative service but as a strategic business partner.

Companies should involve the human resources department in developing and implementing both business and people strategies. This type of partnership is necessary if an organization wants to change potentially inaccurate perceptions of HR and reiterate the HR function's purpose and importance throughout its global environment. Organizations will also discover that HR can be invaluable in facilitating the development of a unifying corporate culture and finding and cultivating much needed leadership talent around the world.

The process of globalizing resources, both human and otherwise, is challenging for any company.

Organizations should realize that their global HR function can help them utilize their existing human talent from across multiple geographic and cultural boundaries. International organizations need to assist and incorporate their HR function to meet the challenges they face if they want to create a truly global workforce.

The globalization of HR is characterized by increasing levels of decentralization. International companies face many challenges when trying to make HR practices consistent across all locations/offices. The top three challenges include:

- Variations in social, political, and economic circumstances.
- Different locations/offices have their own way of doing things and are resistant to change.
- The perceived value of the HR function varies across locations/offices.

Organizations have taken the following actions when trying to create a consistent corporate culture:

- Communicated to all locations about a common corporate culture. Allowed local cultures to maintain their identity in the context of the corporate culture.
- Established common systems (e.g., accounting, marketing, MIS).
- Provided management with education outlining how the company does business.
- Created an organizational mission with input from all

locations.

- Created a written strategy outlining the corporate culture.

1.10.1 General Challenges for Global HR Function: Functions such as operations, sales, and marketing have generally made great progress in adapting to the global reality. However, the HR function has typically lagged behind in developing policies and structures that support globalization. The top challenges HR faces in the globalization process include:

- Coordination of activities in many different locations.
- Understanding the continual change of the globally competitive environment.
- Building a global awareness in all HR departments.
- Creating a multicultural HR team.

1.10.2 International Assignments: Finding, developing, and retaining global leaders tops the priority list of international companies. International, or expatriate, assignments are often used as a way to develop the talent of global leaders.

- Many international companies use expatriate assignments, which last an average of 2.65 years.
- International assignments are quite expensive. Most international companies report spending more than two times an expatriate's salary during the span of the assignment.
- The most important characteristic to look for when recruiting an expatriate is a willingness to travel. The ability to speak other languages was third, behind having international business experience.
- Most organizations provide pre-departure training for expatriates, but relatively few provide a process for managing the expatriate's re-entry to his or her home country.

To conclude, globalization of the economies across the world has changed the notions of manufacturing, productivity and competitiveness. Flexible production processes and structures are being increasingly put in place to compete in very dynamic markets where product life is very short and discerning customers with higher purchasing power and more differentiated and international tastes are demanding much more product variety, higher quality and greater value for money. The new production systems are increasingly moving to the network form of enterprises, each contributing to the production and distribution according to their respective core competencies. Therefore, competitiveness now requires the ability to constantly take the most advantageous position or niche in the rapidly changing market environment.

Globalisation is an irreversible trend and developing economies are also inevitably involved in the process. Developed countries should, therefore, carefully consider how to restructure the world trading system to accommodate developing economies, by enabling them to benefit from globalisation while minimising external shocks. The World Trade Organization (WTO) should work more effectively, through an enlargement of waiver clauses which recognise the weaker position of developing countries.

Despite distortions and aberrations, globalisation is a reality. Developments in information and communication technologies are unifying markets and people, cutting across barriers of space and time. At the end of the day, one has to understand and accept that globalisation is the stratagem for the new millennium. Every country, developed and developing, has to accept this and formulate their economies around it.

2

Human Resources Planning

Human resource planning has traditionally been used by organizations to ensure that the right person is in the right job at the right time. Under past conditions of relative environmental certainty and stability, human resource planning focused on short-term and was dictated largely by line management concerns. Increasing environmental instability, demographic shifts, changes in technology, and heightened international competition are changing the need for and the nature of human resource planning in leading organizations. Planning is increasingly the product of the interaction between line management and planners. In addition, organizations are realizing that in order to adequately address human resource concerns, they must develop long-term as well as short-term solutions. As human resource planners involve themselves in more programs to serve the needs of the business, and even influence the direction of the business, they face new and increased responsibilities and challenges.

In an early treatment of the topic, Vetter (1967) defined human resource planning as the process by which management determines how the organization should move from its current manpower position to its desired position. Through planning, management strives to have the right number and the right kinds of people, at the right places, at the right rime, doing things which result in both the organization and the individual receiving maximum long-run benefits.

Contemporary human resource planning occurs within the broad context of organizational and strategic business planning. It involves forecasting the organization's future human resource needs and planning for how those needs will be met. It includes establishing objectives and then developing and implementing programmes (staffing, appraising, compensating, and training) to ensure that people are available with the appropriate characteristics and skills when and where the organization needs them. It may also involve developing and implementing programs to improve employee performance or to increase employee satisfaction and involvement in order to boost organizational productivity, quality, or innovation (Mills, 1985b). Finally, human resource planning includes gathering data that can be used to evaluate the effectiveness of ongoing programs and inform planners when revisions in their forecasts and programs are needed.

Because a major objective of planning is facilitating an organization's effectiveness, it must be integrated with the organization's short-term and long-term business objectives and plans. Increasingly, this is being done in leading organizations; although in the past, business needs usually defined personnel needs and human resource planning, which meant that planning became a reactive process. The reactive nature of the process went in-hand with a short-term orientation. Now, major changes in business, economic, and social environments are creating uncertainties that are forcing organizations to integrate business planning with human resource planning and to adopt a long-term perspective. For example, according to Kathryn Connors, vice president of human resources at Liz Claiborne,

"Human resources is part of the strategic (business) planning process. It is a part of policy development, line extension planning and the merger and acquisition processes. Little is done in the company that does not involve us in the planning, policy or finalization stages of any deal".

2.1 Reasons for Increased Interest in HR Planning

Undoubtedly, there are many factors that account for the increased attention directed to human resource planning, but environmental forces—globalization, new technologies, economic conditions, and a changing work force—seem particularly potent. These create complexity and uncertainty for organizations. Uncertainty can interfere with efficient operations. Hence, organizations typically attempt to reduce its impact; formal planning is one common tactic used by organizations to buffer themselves from environmental uncertainty.

The changing characteristic of the workforce, which is but one important environmental factor, makes the need for planning evident. These demographic projections have significant implications for managing human resources, thereby increasing the importance of human resource planning. The changing demographics mean there will be fewer entry-level employees, so competition among employers will increase. In addition, the changing demographics signal changes in the abilities, skills, interests, and values of tomorrow's work force.

For example, shortages of many types of skilled workers are imminent, including tool-and-die makers, brick kiln workers, shipbuilders, mechanics, machinists, and engineers. Even if organizations are willing to train new employees, the task may be difficult, as the U.S. Nasty has found. At a time when many of its training manuals required 12th grade reading skills, nearly one fourth of the high school graduates who entered the Navy had studies below the 10th grade level (National Alliance of Business, 1986). Such statistics are alarming when compared to projections indicating that the levels of various skills needed for new jobs are likely to increase in the future.

A consideration of how the values of workers who will soon make up the majority of the workforce differ from those who will begin to leave it, suggests additional changes on the horizon. There is already evidence of growing resistance from employees for relocation. Greater emphasis on self-evaluation and a reduction in loyalty and dedication to employers' makes it more difficult for organizations to assume they can move employees around anywhere and anytime. A decline in organizational loyalty is occurring at the same time when workers are feeling insecure about their employment.

Changes in the workforce is just one aspect of the

environment stimulating the need for human resource planning. The demographic changes are somewhat predictable, but when they are considered in combination with changing technology and many of the other external changes described elsewhere in this issue, they pose significant challenges for human resource planning and contribute to its changing status during the past two decades.

2.2 Short-term HR Planning

Many I/O psychologists work on activities related to designing and implementing programmes (e.g. recruitment, selection systems, and training programs) to meet short-term organizational needs. Such activities generally involve an element of planning in that they are future-oriented to some extent. Even projects for which objectives are expected to be achieved in as little time as a few months have, ideally, been designed with an understanding of how the short-term objectives are linked to the achievement of long-term objectives.

For example, an aeronautics company engaged in a recruitment campaign to hire 100 engineers should have a clear understanding of how this hiring goal will help the company achieve long-term goals such as becoming the world's most innovative company in that industry. This hypothetical company also might have a college recruiting drive designed to find 75 college graduates to enter a training program in recognition of the fact that a growing company needs to prepare for the middle managers—it will need 5 to 7 years hence, as well as for the top level managers, it will need 10 to 15 years. As this hypothetical example highlights, in order for a clear linkage to exist between human resource planning and strategic business planning, it is essential that an organization's top executives have a fully articulated vision for the future, which has been communicated and accepted by managers throughout the organization.

2.3 Forecasting Demand and Supply

In a short-term time horizon, demand and supply of human resources can be predicted with some certainty. Human resource objectives follow logically from consideration of any discrepancies between demand and supply. Demand refers to the number and characteristics (e.g., skills, abilities, pay levels, or experience) of people needed for particular jobs at a given point of time and at a particular place. Supply refers to both the number and characteristics of people available for those particular jobs. Salient questions are: 'What jobs need to be filled (or vacated) during the next 12 months'?, and 'How and where will we get people to fill (or vacate) those jobs'?

The demand question involves predicting who will leave jobs and create vacancies? Which jobs will be eliminated, and which new jobs will be created? One method for pre-dieting both vacancies and job growth is to project historical trends into the future. This is particularly relevant for organizations affected by regular, cyclical fluctuations in demand for their products or services.

The first step in answering this question—the supply question—involves determining the desired characteristics of employees who fill (or vacate) the jobs of interest. Then the availability, of those characteristics in an organization's current workforce and in the external labour market must be assessed. The particular characteristics of current and potential employees that are inventoried and tracked by human resource planners are influenced by the nature of the organization and the environment in which it operates. For example, for human resource planners in growing organizations, simply finding people with the needed skills and abilities is likely to be a top priority. For planners in mature and declining organizations, the costs (e.g. salary level) associated with employees become more salient, especially if workforce reductions are needed. Thus, it is important for the human resource planner to know the business needs and characteristics of the organization. This knowledge is gained by human resource planners meeting with line managers to discuss their business plans as well as their human resource needs. The process of discussion increases the accuracy of supply and demand forecasts and facilitates the establishment of human resource objectives.

2.4 Establishing Objectives

With a short-term horizon, objectives are often easy to state in quantifiable terms. Examples of short-term human resource objectives include increasing the number of people who are attracted to the organization and apply for jobs (increase the applicant pool); attracting a different mix of applicants (with different skills, in different locations, etc.); improving the qualifications of new hires; increasing the length of time that desirable employees stay with the organization; decreasing the length of time that undesirable employees stay with the organization; and helping current and newly hired employees to quickly develop the skills needed by the organization. Such objectives can generally be achieved in a straightforward way by applying state-of-the-art human resource management techniques and working with line managers to ensure agreement with and understanding of the program objectives.

2.5 Long-term HR Planning

Increasingly, long-term human resource planning (for beyond three years) is becoming critical to the effective functioning of organizations. The rapidly changing and highly competitive worldwide marketplace is causing firms to turn to their human resource for survival and competitiveness. Because there is a greater understanding that an organization's workforce cannot be turned around on a dime, long-term human resource planning is gaining currency. It is an activity that demands integration of the skills and knowledge of human resource planner and all the other executives responsible for strategic planning efforts. We use succession planning as our primary example of the process.

More than ever, a major long-term business concern in an organization is, 'What types of managers do we need running into the 21st century, and how do we make sure we have them'? In describing how succession planning efforts differ now from the past, Goodstein (Personal Communication, February 9, 1989) pointed out that the turbulence and unpredictability of the current business environment has resulted in 'a discernible trend' of substituting efforts to define more generic competencies for efforts to identify specific knowledge and skills in the specification of position requirements.

Succession planning programmes are complex systems designed to safeguard the long-term health of the organization. The key activities in succession planning include identifying high-potential employees, identifying needed competencies, and providing learning experiences to develop these competencies. Well-developed programs include a variety of components: selection procedures, development plans, mentorships, frequent and systematic performance reviews, and career planning activities that involve employees in planning and monitoring their own development. Those programs known for their excellence, such as those sponsored by IBM, Exxon, Squibb, and General Electric, represent large investments in integrated human resource management systems. Such programs are examples of what can be done with respect to long-term human resource planning, given the state of our knowledge about human performance in organizational settings, a belief in the value of investing in human resources, and cooperation between the human resource planner and line management.

Staffing the upper echelons of organizations presents a number of unique challenges, particularly when a company practices a promotion-from-within policy. Because the planning horizon is so long, greater uncertainty exists when predicting both future demand and future supply. The uncertainty in predicting supply is compounded by the small numbers of people and jobs involved, which changes the prediction task from one of estimating the percentage of a pool of employees who are likely to be with the company for 'x' years for the future to one of estimating the probability that a few particular individuals will still be with the company 'x' number of years into the future. Providing developmental experiences to a greater number of employees helps reduce the uncertainty of forecasted supply but orchestrating developmental experiences for large numbers of employees can be very difficult logistically, because development is best accomplished by rotating employees through many key jobs throughout their careers. Predicting who will be available and with what capabilities is only half of the problem, of course. Equally challenging is predicting the needs of the organization.

3

Job Evaluation

Once a right candidate is placed on a right job, the person needs to be duly compensated for the job he/she performs. In the pursuit of equal payment, there should be established a consistent and systematic relationship among base compensation rates for all the jobs within the organization. The process of such establishment is termed 'job evaluation'. Different jobs in an organization need to be valued to ascertain their relative worth so that jobs are compensated accordingly and an equitable wage and salary structure is designed in the organization. This is necessary for sustaining cordial relations within and between employees and employer. Hence, there is a need for appreciation of intricacies of the job evaluation in modern organizations. This lesson, as a first step is dedicated to discuss the various fundamental aspects of job evaluation.

3.1 Terminology of Job Evaluation

In the area of job evaluation study, a certain amount of technical terminology is used in order to facilitate communication. It is, therefore, desirable to list and understand allied terms in the job evaluation, as well as some terms that are related to and often confused with job evaluation.

- **Position:** A position is a group of tasks assigned to one individual. There are as many positions in a firm as there are personnel.
- **Job:** Edwin B. Flippo describes job as a group of positions that are similar as to kind and level of work. In some instances, only one position may be involved, simply because no other similar position exists. For example, in the typical firm the position of human resource manager also constitutes a job since there is only one human

resource manager in the organization.

- **Job Analysis:** It is the process of studying and collecting information relating to the operations and responsibilities of a specific job. The immediate products of this analysis are job descriptions and job specifications.
- **Motion Study:** This also involves study of the job. Motions study is one of the ways of studying job. It is a process of analyzing a job to find the easiest, most effective, and most economical method of doing it. As such, motion study is a part of the job design function.
- **Job Description:** It is an organized, factual statement of the duties and responsibilities of a specific job. In brief, it should tell what is to be done, how it is to be done, and why it is to be done. It is a standard of function, in that it defines the appropriate and authorized content of a job.
- **Job Specification:** It is a statement of the minimum acceptable human qualities necessary to perform a job properly. It is a standard of personnel and designates the qualities required for acceptable performance.
- **Evaluation:** Wigley explains evaluation as a data reduction process that involves the collection of large amount of data which are analyzed and synthesized into an overall judgment of worth or merit. The implication here is that the judgment of worth can be supported by the data. In her review, Foxon found similar definitions referring to judgments of value or worth.
- **Job Evaluation:** It is a systematic and orderly process of determining the worth of a job in relation to other jobs. The objective of this process is to determine the correct rate of pay. It is, therefore, not the same as job analysis. Rather, it follows the job analysis process, which provides the basic data to be evaluated.

In simple worlds, job evaluation is the rating of jobs in an organization. This is the process establishing the value or worth of jobs in a job hierarchy and compares the relative intrinsic value or worth of jobs within an organization. Some renowned definitions of job evaluation are described below.

Scott, Clothier and Priegel defined job evaluation as "the operation of evaluating a particular job in relation to other jobs either within or outside the organization".

Dale Yoder described job evaluation as "a practice which seeks to provide a degree of objectivity in measuring the comparative value of jobs within an organization and among similar organizations".

Edwin B. Flippo defined job evaluation as "a systematic and orderly process of determining the worth of a job in relation to other jobs".

Arthur A. Sloane described job evaluation as "any formalized system that attempts to determine the relative worth of different jobs in the organization so that jobs of greater value can be rewarded by greater pay".

According to the International Labour Organization (ILO), "job evaluation is an attempt to determine and compare the demands which the normal performance of a particular job makes on normal workers, without taking into account the individual abilities or performance of the workers concerned".

The British Institute of Management defines job evaluation "as the process of analysis and assessment of jobs to ascertain reliably their negative worth using the assessment as the basis for a balanced wage structure".

Wendell French defines job evaluation as "a process of determining the relative worth of the various jobs within the organization, so that differential wages may be paid to jobs of different worth.

The relative worth of a job means relative value produced. The variables which are assumed to be related to value produced are such factors as responsibility, skill, effort and working conditions".

3.2 Objectives of Job Evaluation

The main objective of job evaluation is to ensure equitable remuneration for relative worth of a job. As per the ILO

Report, the aim of the majority of systems of job evaluation is to establish, on agreed logical basis, the relative values of different jobs in a given plant or machinery, i.e., it aims at determining the relative worth of a job. The principle upon which all job evaluation schemes are based is that of describing and assessing the value of all jobs in the firms in terms of a number of factors, the relative importance of which varies from job to job".

The objectives of job evaluation, to put in a more systematic manner are to:

1. Establish a standard procedure for determining the relative worth of each job in an organization.
2. Ensure equitable wage for a job and reasonable wage differentials between different jobs in a hierarchical organization.
3. Determine the rate of pay for each job which is fair and equitable with relation to other jobs in the plant, community or industry.
4. Eliminate wage inequalities.
5. Use as a basis for fixing incentives and different bonus plans.
6. Promote a fair and accurate consideration of all employees for advancement and transfer.
7. Provide information for work organization, employees' selection, placement, training and other similar purposes.
8. Provide a benchmark for making career planning for the employees in the organization.

3.3 Principles of Job Evaluation

The job evaluation has certain principles. These principles are supposed to be kept in the mind by the job evaluators. These principles are not only directives of proper job evaluation but also provide clarity in the process of evaluation. According to Kress, these principles are:

1. Rate the job and the jobber. Each element should be rated on the basis of what the job itself requires;

2. The elements selected for rating purposes should be easily explainable in terms and a few in numbers as will cover the necessary requisites for every job without any overlapping;
3. The elements should be clearly defined and properly selected;
4. Any job rating plan must be sold to foremen and employees. The success in selling it will depend on a clear-cut explanation and illustration of the plan;
5. Foreman should participate in the rating of jobs in their own departments;
6. Maximum co-operation can be obtained from employees when they themselves have an opportunity to discuss job ratings; and
7. Too many occupational wages should not be established. It would be unwise to adopt an occupational wage for each total of point values.

3.4 Job Evaluation Criteria

The system of job evaluation utilizes a total of eight measurement factors. The various factors analyse a position in relation to the skills and experience required for competent performance, the demands made on the job and the overall structure and responsibility/accountability involved. A point rating is derived for each factor and the sum of these points represents the total point's value of the job.

3.4.1 Basic Evaluation Rules: The basic rules for evaluating each position are:

1. The current position is evaluated without being influenced by what the job is likely to be in the future or what it may have been in the past.
2. The position is evaluated and not the job holder. The assessment of each factor is based on the job being performed competently. The assessment of the job holder's own performance against the standard required is a quite separate exercise which is outside the scope of the job evaluation rating.

3.4.2 Job Evaluation Factors: The job evaluation system

comprises the following factors. In some cases, minor changes to the wording are used to define factors and levels made in order to better align the methodology with the client's culture and environment. Where this is done, great care is taken to ensure that inter-organisation consistency is not compromised. The primary factor in determining compensation is the evaluation of work performed. The internal worth of a job is evaluated based upon factor like know-how, problem solving, and accountability, education, experience, complexity involved in the job, scope of job, supervision received and, authority exercised.

A. Know-How: The knowledge, skill and experience required for standard acceptable performance. It considers the requirement for technical and professional skills, expertise and experience, the amount of planning and organising required and the requirement to work with and through others.

B. Problem Solving: The thinking required for analysing, evaluating, creating, reasoning, arriving at and drawing conclusions; the extent to which this thinking is covered by precedents or circumscribed by standards; and the degree of creativity or original thought required.

C. Accountability: The degree to which the employee is held accountable for taking action and for the consequences of that action. It is the measured effect of the job on end results—the freedom to act measured through the existence or absence of constraints by managers, committees and procedures and the impact of that action on the organization.

D. Education: The level of formal education required to perform the functions required of a position. There is often an overlap between education and experience, and for this reason it is often advisable to consider the education level that would be expected of a new incumbent recruited externally.

E. Experience: The length of practical experience and nature of technical/managerial familiarity required. This experience is in addition to formal education.

F. Complexity: Measured in terms of: (a) the time taken to learn and adjust to specific job requirements, (b) the level to which the job functions are defined and follow established and predictable patterns, and (c) the thinking challenge required to adapt to rapidly changing circumstances and innovative or conceptual thinking needed to initiate new corporate direction.

G. Scope of Job: The complexity and scope of work factors tend to be related to the education and experience level required of a position. The calculation of points for each of these factors is based on the application of a percentage rating of the sum of the points derived in the evaluation of education and experience.

H. Supervision Received: The extent of supervision, direction or guidance imposed on the job holder and the freedom that the executive has to take action.

I. Authority Exercised: Authority level expressed in terms of routine expenditure, capital expenditure and investments, granting of loans, hiring and firing staff, etc.

3.5 Job Evaluation Processes

Job evaluation is a technique to rank jobs in an organization on the basis of the duties and responsibilities assigned to the job. The job evaluation process results in a job being assigned to a pay grade. The pay grade is associated with a pay range that is defined by a minimum and a maximum pay rate. A model of job evaluation process with the following steps is presented below.

- **Step 1-Job Description:** The position supervisor assigns duties and writes the job description. If there is an incumbent employee, s/he reviews it, and they both sign it. Instructions and additional assistance are available from human resources department, if needed. The job description is a snapshot of the job as it presently exists, reflecting the current duties and responsibilities of the job and/or the incumbent.
- **Step 2-Approval:** The vice president reviews job descriptions and, s/he concurs, approves the responsibilities, requirements, and departmental organization contained

within a job description presented for new evaluation, and signs it. If the vice president does not concur with the contents of the description, it is returned to the supervisor for changes.

- **Step 3-Review:** Human resources review the job description as submitted with the supervisor prior to evaluation by the job evaluation committee (Step 4). Human resources ensure that there is consistency and equity in the job description and titles by editing them for clarity and format. If the human resources office makes changes, the job description is returned to the supervisor and vice president for signature prior to being presented to the job evaluation committee (Step 4).
- **Step 4-Evaluation:** The job evaluation committee (JEC) is a multimember committee, the members of which are appointed by the staff salary administration committee (SSAC), representing employees throughout the organization. JEC ensures equity among jobs through the use of established, consistent criteria for evaluation and prevents escalation of the job evaluation grades by validating changes in job content presented for review. Members of JEC receive in-depth training on job evaluation and utilize a consistently applied points system for the evaluations.
- **Step 5-Confirmation:** SSAC confirms all job evaluations and titles recommended by JEC. This committee is composed of the SLCC vice presidents, the human resources director, and other relevant experts. After confirmation of the evaluation job description, SSAC advises the supervisor of the results of the evaluation and the title. The supervisor then advises the employee of the results of the job evaluation.

3.6 Methods of Job Evaluation

A number of job evaluation methods have been developed since the 1920s, and many, if not most, of them are still used.

They all have the same final objective—ranking jobs in terms of their relative worth to the organization so that an equitable rate of pay can be determined for each job. As the job evaluation is mostly a judgmental process that would probably use one of the job evaluation methods, commonly grouped into two major categories: quantitative and non-quantitative. The basic difference between these two methods lies in the sense that, under non-quantitative methods, a job is compared as a whole with other jobs in the organization, whereas in case of quantitative methods, the key factors of a job are selected and then measured. The most commonly used non-quantitative methods are ranking and job classification or grading method, while the most common quantitative methods are factor comparison and point rating. The starting point for all job evaluation methods is a current job description and job specification.

3.6.1 Non-quantitative Methods: Non-quantitative methods call for the evaluation of a whole job relative to the other jobs or to the general descriptions of jobs within an organization. For instance, a job description of a customer service representative may be compared to the job description of a word processing specialist. The main role of the evaluator is to determine which of the jobs is more important or worth more to the organization. The major types of non-quantitative job evaluation procedures are ranking and job classification.

3.6.2 Ranking Method of Job Evaluation: This is the simplest form of job evaluation method. The method involves ranking each job relative to all other jobs, usually based on some overall factors like 'job difficulty'. Each job as a whole is compared with other and this comparison of jobs goes on until all the jobs have been evaluated and ranked. All jobs are ranked in the order of their importance from the simplest to the hardest or from the highest to the lowest. The importance of order of job is judged in terms of duties, responsibilities and demands on the job holder. The following steps are involved in ranking jobs.

- **Obtain Job Information:** The first step is job analysis. Job descriptions for each job are prepared and these are the basis on which the rankings are made. The job ranking method usually ranks jobs according to 'the whole job' rather than a number of compensable factors.
- **Select Raters and Jobs to be Rated:** Ranking all the jobs, at a time, is usually not possible. The more usual procedure involves ranking jobs by department or in 'clusters' i.e. factory workers, clerical workers and so on. This eliminates the need for having to compare directly, say, factory jobs and clerical jobs.
- **Select Compensable Factors:** In the ranking method, it is common to use just one factor, for instance, job difficulty, and to rank jobs on the basis of 'the whole job'. Regardless of the number of factors you choose, it is advisable to carefully explain the definition of the factor(s) to the evaluators so that they evaluate the jobs consistently.
- **Rank Jobs:** Next, the jobs are ranked. The simplest way to do this involves giving each rater a set of index cards, each of which contains a brief descript of a job. These cards are then ranked from lowest to highest.
- **Combine Rating:** It is usually to have several raters rank the jobs independently. Finally, divide all the ranked jobs into appropriate groups or classifications by considering the common features of jobs such as similar duties, skills, or knowledge required. All the jobs within a particular group or classification receive the same wage or range of raters. Then, once this is accomplished, the rating committee can simply average the ranking.

Ranking method has the following merits in terms of its procedure, resources involvement and operational mechanisms.

1. It is the simplest method.
2. It is quite economical to put it into effect.
3. It is less time consuming and involves little paper work.

The ranking method has the following demerits in terms of validity and reliability.

1. The main demerit of the ranking method is that there are no definite standards of judgment and also there is no way of measuring the differences between jobs.
2. It suffers from its sheer unmanageability when there are a large number of jobs.

3.6.3 Job Classification or Grading Method: This is a simple, widely used method. This method of job evaluation was made popular by the U.S. Civil Service Commission. In the ranking system, there is no re-determined yardstick of values. In the job grading approach, there is one such yardstick constituting of job classes or grades. Jobs are measured as whole jobs. Under this method, job grades or classes are established by an authorised body or committee appointed for this purpose. A job grade is defined as a group of different jobs of similar difficulty or requiring similar skills to perform them. Job grades are determined on the basis of information derived from job analysis. The example of job grades may include, depending on the type of jobs the organization offers, skilled, unskilled, account clerk, clerk-cum typist, steno-typist, office superintendent, laboratory assistant and so on.

There are several ways to categorize jobs. One is to draw up 'class description and place jobs into classes based on their correspondence to these descriptions. Another is to draw up a set of classifying rules for each class and then categorize the jobs according to these rules. The usual procedure is to choose compensable factors and then develop class or grade descriptions that describe each class in terms of amount or level of compensable factor(s) in jobs. Such factors are:

1. Difficultly and variety of work.
2. Supervision received and exercised.
3. Judgment exercised.
4. Originality required.
5. Nature and purpose of interpersonal work relationships.
6. Responsibility.
7. Experience.
8. Knowledge required.

The following five steps are generally involved in the process of job classification.

1. Prepare job description for basic information about he job.
2. Prepare job grading description for identification of different levels of jobs. Each grade level must be distinct from the grade level adjacent to it. After establishing the grade level, each job is assigned to an appropriate grade level on the basis of the complexity of duties, non-supervisory responsibilities and supervisory responsibilities.
3. Select grades and key jobs (about 10 to 20 jobs), which include all the major departments and functions and cover all the grades.
4. Grade the key jobs. Key jobs are assigned to an appropriate grade level and their relationship to each other is studied.
5. Classify all the jobs on the basis of grade definitions. All the jobs in the same grade receive the same wage or range of rate. For instance, menials may be put into one class; clerks in another; junior officers in a higher class; and the top executives in the top class.

The job classification method has several advantages. The major merits of the method are:

1. This method is easy to understand and simple to operate.
2. It is economical and therefore, suitable for small organizations.
3. The grouping of jobs into classifications makes pay determination problems easy to administer.
4. This method is useful for government jobs.

The job classification method also has some disadvantages. The major demerits of the method are:

1. The method suffers from personal bias of the committee members.
2. It cannot deal with complex jobs which will not fit neatly into one grade.
3. This method is rarely used in industries.
4. It is difficult to know how much of a job's rank is influenced by the man on the job.

5. The system is rather rigid and unsuitable for large organizations or for very varied work.

3.6.4 Quantitative Methods: Quantitative methods divide jobs into component parts and require absolute or relative value judgements about how much of a component part a particular job requires. The two most popular types of quantitative systems are the point rating and factor comparison methods.

A. Point Rating Method: This is the most widely used system of job evaluation. The method evaluates the compensable factors of each job. It involves a more detailed, quantitative and analytical approach to the measurement of job work. Under this method, jobs are broken down, based on various identifiable factors such as skill, effort, training, knowledge, hazards, responsibilities and so on. Thereafter, points are allocated to each of these factors. Weights are given to factors depending on their importance to perform the job. Points so allocated to various factors of a job are then summed. Then, the jobs with similar total of points are placed in similar pay grades. The sum of points gives an index of the relative significance of the jobs that are rated.

This system requires six steps and is usually implemented by a job evaluation committee or by an individual analyst.

1. **Determine Critical Factors:** The points rating method includes the following job factors for allocation of points: (a) safety of other, (b) equipment of materials, (c) assisting trainees, and (d) production or service quality.
2. **Determine the Levels of Factors:** Since, the amount of responsibility or other factors may vary from job to job, the point rating method rates several levels associated with each factor. These levels help analysts reward different degrees of responsibility, skill, and other critical factors.
3. **Allocate Points to Sub-factors:** With the factors listed down one side and the levels placed across the top, the result is a point method matrix. Starting with the highest level, the job evaluation committee subjectively assigns

the maximum possible points to each sub-factor. The allocation allows the committee to give very precise weights to each element of the job.

4. **Allocate Points to Levels:** Once the total points for each job element are assigned under the highest level, analysts allocate points across each row to reflect the importance of the different levels.
5. **Develop Points Manually:** Analysts then develop a point manual. It contains a written explanation of each job element. It also defines what is expected for the various levels of each sub-factor. This information is needed to assign jobs to their appropriate levels.
6. **Apply the Point System:** When the point matrix and manual are ready, the relative value of each job can be determined. This process is subjective. It requires specialists to compare job descriptions with the point manual for each sub-factor. The match between the job description and the point manual statement reveals the level and points for each sub-factor of every job. The points for each sub-factor are added to find the total number of points for the job. After the total points for each job are known, the jobs are ranked.

The points rating have several advantages. The major merits of the method are:

1. It is the most comprehensive and accurate method of job evaluation.
2. Prejudice and human judgement are minimised. The method cannot be manipulated.
3. Being a systematic method, workers in the organization favour this method.
4. The scales developed in this method can be used for long time.
5. Jobs can be easily placed in distinct categories.

The points rating method also has some disadvantages. The major demerits of the method are:

1. It is both time-consuming and an expensive method.

2. It is difficult to understand for an average worker.
3. A lot of clerical work is involved in recording rating scales.
4. It is not suitable for managerial jobs wherein the work content is not measurable in quantitative terms.

B. Factors Comparison Method: This is a combination of both rating and point rating methods. It rates jobs by comparing them and makes analysis by breaking jobs into compensable factors. This system is usually used to evaluate white collar, professional and managerial positions. The mechanism for evaluating jobs under this method involves the flowing steps.

- **Determine the Compensable Factors:** Analysts must first decide which factors are common and important in a broad range of jobs. The critical factors like responsibility, skill, mental efforts, physical effort and working conditions are most commonly used. Some organizations use different factors for managerial, professional, sales, and other types of jobs.
- **Determine Key Jobs:** Key jobs are those that are commonly found throughout the organization and are common in the employer's market. Common jobs are selected because it is easier to discover the market rate for them. Ideally, these benchmark jobs should be accepted by employee as key jobs and should encompass a wide variety of critical factors to be evaluated. Typically, 10-25 key jobs are selected by the committee.
- **Allocate Present Wages for Key Jobs:** The job evaluation committee then allocates a part of each key job's current wage rate to each critical factor. The proportion wage assigned to each of the different compensable factors depends on the importance of the factor. The base rate is agreed upon by the company.
- **Place Key Jobs on a Factor Comparison Chart:** Once the wage rates are assigned to the compensable factors of each key job, this information is transferred to a factor

comparison chart. Key job titles are placed in the factor columns according to the rate of wages assigned to the job for each critical factor.

- **Evaluate Other Jobs:** The titles of key jobs in each column of the factor comparison chart serve as benchmarks; other non-key jobs are then evaluated by fitting them in the rate scale under each factor column.

The factors' comparison has several advantages. The major merits are:

1. It is a more objective method of job evaluation.
2. The method is flexible as there is no upper limit on the rating.
3. It is a fairly easy method to explain to employees.
4. The use of limited number of factors (usually five) ensures less chances of overlapping and over-weighting of factors.
5. It facilitates determining the relative worth of different jobs.

The factors comparison method also has some disadvantages. The major demerits of the method are:

1. It is an expensive and time consuming method.
2. Using the same five factors for evaluating jobs may not always be appropriate because jobs differ across and within the organization.
3. It is difficult to understand and operate.

3.7 Limitations/Drawbacks of Job Evaluation

In spite of many advantages, job evaluation suffers from the following drawbacks/limitations.

1. Job evaluation is susceptible because of human error and subjective judgement. While there is no standard list of factors to be considered for job evaluation, there are some factors that cannot be measured accurately.
2. There is a variation between wages fixed through job evaluation and by market forces. Say Kerr and Fisher, the jobs which tend to rate high as compared with the market are those of junior, nurse and typist, while craft rates are

relatively low. Weaker groups are better served by an evaluation plan then by the market, the former places the emphasis not only on force but on equity.

3. When job evaluation is applied for the first time in an organization, it creates doubts in the minds of workers whose jobs are evaluated and trade unions that it may do away with collective bargaining for fixing wage rates.
4. Job evaluation methods, lacking in scientific basis, are often looked upon as suspicious as regards their efficacy.
5. Job evaluation is a time-consuming process requiring specialised technical personnel to undertake it and, thus, is likely to be costly.
6. Job evaluation is not found suitable for establishing the relative worth of the managerial jobs which are skill-oriented. However, these skills cannot be measured in quantitative terms.

4

Performance Appraisal Techniques

In almost every organization, every employee is subjected to periodic appraisal of his/her performance. This is highly important if the organization's human resource development objectives are to be realized, if the organization wants to make best use of its human resource available and if the organization wants to have a scientific and retinal compensation system. An effective performance appraisal system brings rationality in management. If an organization wants to maximize its effectiveness then the organization must have tool by which it can discriminate between an effective employee and a not so effective employee. Today, appraisal is not something of a choice left to the wishes of the corporate bosses, nor it is a privilege to be enjoyed by few businesses conglomerates.

Therefore, it is a must for every organization for its survival and growth. The appraisal practices are in some cases structured and formally sanctioned and in other instances, they are an informal and integral part of daily activities. Thus, across human activities someway or the other, performance appraisal is conducted in different ways and all of us, consciously or unconsciously evaluate our own actions from time to time. In social situation, performance is conducted in a systematic and planned manner to achieve various organizational goals in a social system.

4.1 Background of Performance Appraisal

Performance appraisal is not something new. The appraisal system existed as early as 221 A.D., though the nature of appraisal was not so formal and the tools used were not so scientific. In fact, the appraisal gained momentum in the post-Second World War period with the advent of professionalization in management. In the early stages, the performance appraisal was done just on the basis of the degree to which a person possessed certain traits, which were considered essential for effective performance of a particular task. Performance appraisal of individuals, groups and organizations is a common practice among all the societies.

The history of performance appraisal is quite brief. Its roots in the early 20th century can be traced to Taylor's pioneering time and motion studies. But this is not very helpful—for the same might be said about almost everything in the field of modern human resources management. As a distinct and formal management procedure of evaluation of work performance, appraisal system was since the time of the Second World War. Yet in a broader sense, the practice of appraisal of employee's performance in different work places is a very ancient art. Dulewicz says that a basic human tendency is to make judgments about one's own work, as well as about oneself. Appraisal, it seems, is both inevitable and universal for human activities. In the absence of a carefully structured system of appraisal, people will tend to judge the work performance of others, including subordinates, naturally, informally and arbitrarily.

The human inclination to judge can create serious motivational, ethical and legal problems in the workplace. Without a structured appraisal system, there is little chance of ensuring that the judgments made will be lawful, fair, defensible and accurate. Performance appraisal systems began as simple methods of income justification. That is, appraisal was used to decide whether or not the salary or wage of an individual employee was justified. The process was firmly linked to material outcomes. If an employee's performance was found to be less than ideal, a cut in pay would follow.

On the other hand, if their performance was better than the supervisor expected, a pay rise was in order. As a result, the traditional emphasis on reward outcomes was progressively rejected. In the 1950s, in the United States, the potential usefulness of appraisal as a tool for motivation and development was gradually recognized. The general model of performance appraisal, as it is known today, began from that time. Although the interest in the use of performance appraisal has increased over the last thirty years, the practice of formally evaluating employees' has existed for centuries. The performance appraisal system has undergone a lot of changes over the years as shown in Table 4.1.

Table 4.1: Gradual Progress of Performance Appraisal System

Period	Development
1900	Subjective
1940	Increased Psychometric Sophistication
1950	Management by Objectives (MBO)
1960	BARS
1970-1990	Hybrid System and Approach
Beyond 2000	360 Degree Appraisal

4.2 Terminological Clarity

There are some terms in usage among the practitioners as well writers, which are used for assessment of job and jobber at workplace, such as performance appraisal, potential appraisal, performance management and job evaluation. For better understanding of the performance appraisal, let us have clarity and differences among these terms.

- **Job Evaluation:** It is clear to us from the pervious chapter that job evaluation is systematic and orderly and determines the value/worth of a job to determine wage levels for different jobs. It rates a job keeping in view of the responsibilities, qualification, experience, working conditions required to perform a job.
- **Potential Appraisal:** It is an appraisal of a person's present competencies, which are not applied on the present job. Thus, inner potentiality is identified keeping in mind the future job roles of a person.
- **Performance Management:** It is consolidation of goal

setting, performance appraisal, and development into a single, common system. The aim of the performance management is to insure that employee's performance is supporting the organization's strategic aims.

- **Merit Rating:** It is a systematic, periodic and, so far as humanly possible, an impartial rating of an employee's excellence in matters pertaining to his present job and to his potentialities for a job.
- **Performance Appraisal:** It is evaluating an employee's current and/or past performance relative to his or her performance standards.

4.3 Concept of Performance Appraisal

In the context of an industrial organization, performance appraisal is a systematic evaluation of personnel by supervisors or those familiar with their performance. In other words, performance appraisal is a systematic and objective way of judging the relative worth or ability of an employee in performing his/her task.

Many authors described and some of them tried to define the concept of performance appraisal in their own way. According to Gary Dessler, performance appraisal is an evaluation of employee's current or past performance relative to his/her performance standards. Further, he mentioned that the appraisal process involves three steps:

1. Setting work standards.
2. Assessing the employee's actual performance relative to these standards.
3. Providing feedback to the employee with the aim of motivating that person to eliminate performance deficiencies or to continue to perform above par.

McGregor discusses the formal performance appraisal plans in view of meeting three needs—out of which one is relating to organization and other two for individual. The first one, organization level, is to provide systematic judgments to back up salary increases, transfers, demotions, or terminations.

The other two, individual level, are relating to certain means which are meant for subordinates to tell them how boss is doing, and suggesting desired changes in behaviour, attitude, skills or job knowledge. This can be used to make subordinate to know the level of performance standards and use them as a base for coaching and counselling the individual employee.

Performance appraisal may be defined as a structured formal interaction between a subordinate and supervisor, that usually takes the form of a periodic interview (annual or semi-annual), in which the work performance of the subordinate is examined and discussed, with a view to identifying weaknesses and strengths as well as opportunities for improvement and skill development.

Appraising the performance is a method of evaluating the behaviour of employees in the work spot, normally including both the quantitative and qualitative aspects of job performance. Performance refers to the degree of accomplishment of the tasks that make up an individual's job. It includes how well an individual is fulfilling the job demands. In order to find out whether an employee is worthy of continued employment or not, and if so, whether he should receive a pay rise or promotion, performance needs to be evaluated from time to time.

It is by and large useful not only for different payment purposes but also to make aware of one's strengths and weaknesses. This is useful because employees would then be able to understand which area they are supposed to improve their performance. Under this exercise, evaluation is not only the performance of a worker in the job but also his/her employee potential for development as regards future job roles. Moreover, performance appraisals should focus on work planning and continuous review for development. They should also focus on quality to survive in the current environment.

Every organization has to decide upon the content to be appraised before the programme is approved. Generally, content to be appraised is determined on the basis of job analysis. Contents to be appraised are in the form of contribution to organizational objectives like production, cost saving, return on capital so on. Other measures include behaviour which means observable physical actions and movements, objectives which measure job related results like amount of deposits mobilized, and traits which measures in terms of personal characteristics observable in employee's job activities. The contents to be appraised may vary with the purpose of appraisal and type and level of employee. There are different methods designed and experimented in this regard.

Alford and Beatty define performance appraisal as, 'the evaluation or appraisal of the relative worth of a jobber's (person's) services on his/her job to the organization'.

According to Dale Beach, performance appraisal is the systematic evaluation of the individual with regard to his or her performance on the job and his potential for development. Beach has identified changes in performance appraisal that have taken place since 1920s. These are summarized in Table 4.2.

Table 4.2: Trends in Performance Appraisal

Element	Earlier Emphasis	Present Emphasis
Terminology	Merit rating	Employee appraisal/ performance appraisal
Purpose	Determining qualifications for wage increase, transfer, promotion, lay-off	Development of personnel, improved performance on the job, and providing emotional security
Application	Hourly-paid workers	Technical, professional and managerial personnel
Factors Rated	Heavy emphasis on personal attributes	Results, accomplishments, performance
Techniques	Rating scales, statistical manipulation of data for comparison purposes	Mutual goal setting, critical incidents, group appraisal, performance standards, less quantitative

4.4 Objectives of Performance Appraisal

Performance appraisals consist of a systematic, face-to-face discussion of an employee's work performance, training and development needs, future job goals and job aspirations. It looks backwards, reviewing the employee's performance during the period under review, and forward, helping the employee prepare and set goals for the upcoming review period. To be effective, performance appraisal programmes must be linked closely to corporate goals and objectives, including departmental business plans. Primary objectives are:

1. Performance review.
2. Identification of training and development needs.
3. Setting work objectives.
4. Employee performance counselling.
5. Employee career planning.
6. Employee remuneration/recognition reviews.

Performance appraisal serves the following management objectives:

1. **Providing Basis for Promotion/Transfer/Termination:** Identifying those subordinates who deserve promotion or require lateral shift or termination which can be used for career planning.
2. **Enhancing Employee's Effectiveness:** Helping an employee, by identifying strengths and weaknesses and informing him as to what performance is expected from him/her which would go a long way in making him understand his role well.
3. **Identifying Employee's Training and Developmental Needs:** Identifying training and development needs of employees is necessary to prepare them for meeting challenges in their current and future employment roles.
4. **Removing Work Alienation:** Identifying and removing factors responsible for workers' discontent which would motivate them for better work performance. Performance appraisal helps in creating a positive and healthy climate in the organization.
5. **Developing Inter-personal Relationship:** Relation between superiosr-subordinates can be improved through realization that each is dependent on the other for better performance and success. By facilitating employees to do

introspection, self-evaluation and goal setting, their behaviour can be modified. Better inter-personal relationship leads to team-building.

6. **Removing Discontent:** Identifying and removing factors responsible for workers' discontent would motivate them for better work performance. Performance appraisal helps in creating a positive and healthy climate.
7. **Removing Worker Alienation:** Counselling of employees corrects misreading which might result in work alienation. Performance appraisal helps in creating a positive and healthy climate in the organization.

Wayne and Kacmar, stated that the assessment areas differ from organization to organization and from job to job. Depending on the requirements of a job, the department and the organization, some typical assessment areas include:

- Quality/accuracy of work.
- Quantity of output.
- Ability to make decisions.
- Job knowledge.
- Technical and job related skills.
- Attendance and punctuality.
- Ability to work as a member of a team.
- Future potential/ability to work in other areas.
- Training and development needs.
- Commitment to safety.
- Dependability.

4.5 Performance Appraisal Process

The performance appraisal process starts with employee planning and ends with an evaluation of employee progress. The performance appraisal process consists of broadly two steps. First, complete the performance appraisal form, and secondly, participate in a performance appraisal interview and discussion. These two stages comprise the following levels in appraising the performance of the staff.

1. **Establish Performance Standards or Goals:** The appraisal process begins with the establishment of performance standards. The officers must determine what outputs, accomplishments and skills will be evaluated. These standards should evolve out of job analysis and job description. These performance standards should be clear and objectives are to be understood and measured.
2. **Communicate Performance Expectations to Employees**: Once the performance standards are established, these need to be communicated to the respective employees so that they come to know what is expected of them. Past experience indicates that not communicating standards to the employees compounds the appraisal problems. Here, it must be noted that mere transfer of information from the officer to the staff is not communication. It becomes communication only when the transfer of information has taken place and has been received and well understood by the staff. The feedback from the staff on the standards communicated to them must be obtained. If required, the standards may be modified or revised in the light of feedback obtained from the employees. It is important to note that communication is a two-way street.
3. **Measure Actual Performance:** This is the third step involved in the appraisal process. In this stage, the actual performance of the employee's is measured on the basis of information available from various sources such as personal observation, statistical reports, oral reports, and written reports. The evaluator's feeling should not influence the performance measurements of the staff. Measurement must be objective, based on facts and findings. This is because what we measure is more critical and important to the evaluation process than how we measure.
4. **Compare Actual Performance with Standards:** In this stage, the actual performance is compared with the pre-determined standards. Such a comparison may reveal the

deviation between standard performance and actual performance and will enable the evaluator to proceed to the fifth step on the process i.e. review and discussion of the appraisal with the concerned staff.

5. **Discuss and Review the Appraisal with the Staff:** The fifth step in the appraisal process is to communicate to and discuss with the employees, the results of the appraisal. This is one of the most challenging tasks the officers face—to present an accurate appraisal to the staff and then make them accept the appraisal in a constructive manner. A discussion on appraisal enables employees to know their strengths and weaknesses. This, in turn, does impact their future performance. The impact may be positive or negative depending upon how the appraisal is presented and discussed with the employees'. Steps in a performance review are follows:

- Clarify job description and responsibilities.
- Clarify employee development interests and needs.
- List specific development areas for concentration.
- Review performance objectives and performance standards.
- Review progress towards objectives through ongoing feedback and periodic discussions.
- Decide on purpose(s). Typically, the purposes include giving employees answers to: What am I expected to do? How well am I doing? What are my strengths and weaknesses? How can I do a better job? How can I contribute more?

6. **Initiate Corrective Action:** The final step in the appraisal process is the initiation of corrective action when it is necessary. The areas needing improvement are identified and then, the measures to correct or improve the performance are identified and initiated.

4.6 Methods of Performance Appraisal

Methods of performance are described as those which can

be used to measure and appraise employee's performance. There are a good number of methods which are available. In fact, each organization has its own suitable method for performance appraisal. Each method with its strengths and weaknesses may be suited for one organization and non-suitable for another organization. As such, there is no single appraisal method accepted and used by all organizations to measure their employees' performance.

4.6.1 Categories of Performance Appraisal Methods: All the methods of appraisal devised so far have been classified differently by different authors. DeCenzo and Robbins have classified appraisal methods into three categories: absolute methods, relevant methods and objective methods. Aswathappa has classified these into two categories: past-oriented and future-oriented. Michael R. Carrell has classified all appraisal methods into as many as six categories: sales, comparative methods, critical incidents, essay, MBO and combination and methods. Rock and Levis have classified the methods into two broad categories: narrow interpretation and broad interpretation. Beatty and Sclceier have categorised various methods of appraisal into four groups: comparative methods, absolute methods, goal setting, and direct indices.

A more widely used classification of appraisal methods consists of two categories—traditional methods and modern methods, given by Strauss and Sayles. Traditional methods lay emphasis on the rating of the individual's personality traits, such as initiative, dependability, drive, creativity, integrity, intelligence, leadership potential and so on. The modern methods place more emphasis on the evaluation of work results, i.e. job achievements, than the personal traits. Modern methods tend to be more objective and worthwhile.

4.7 Selection of Performance Appraisal Method

The choice of method should be based largely on the purpose of appraisal. There are a variety of methods available to appraise performance in different dimensions. As discussed above, these methods are classified into two categories, viz., traditional methods and modem methods. Strengths and weaknesses of these methods were analyzed on the basis of certain dimensions. Under each dimension, how each method works, is also presented in a comprehensive manner. These categories and associated methods are briefly discussed below.

4.7.1 Traditional Methods: These are as under:

A. Rankings Method: It is the oldest and simplest method of performance appraisal, by which a man and his performance are considered as an entity by the rater. No attempt is made to fractionalize the rate or his performance; the 'whole man' is compared with the 'whole man'. It involves raking all employees, according to job performance and commitment to the organization. It is the oldest and simplest formal systematic method of performance appraisal in which one employee is compared with all others for the purpose of placing them in a simple rank order. The staff can be ranked from the highest to the lowest or from the best to the worst. The relative position of each employee is tested in terms of his numerical rank. It may also be done by ranking a person on his job performance against that of another member of a competitive group by placing him as a number one or two or three in the total group.

The greatest limitation of this method is that in practice, it is very difficult to compare a single individual with human beings having varying behaviour traits. The method only tells us how a man stands in relation to the others in the group but does not indicate how much better or worse he is than the other.

B. Paired Comparison Method: In this method, each employee is compared with other employees on one-on-one basis—usually based on one trait only. The rater is provided with a bunch of slips each containing a pair of names; the rater puts a tick mark against the employee whom he considers the better of the two. The number of times this employee is compared as better with others determines his or her final ranking.

4.7.2 Modern Methods: As we have understood, most

traditional methods emphasize either on the task or the worker's personality, while making an appraisal. In order to bring about a balance between these two, modern methods have been developed. These methods are briefly discussed below.

BARS (Behavioural Anchored Rating Scale): The problem of judgemental evaluation inherent in the traditional methods of performance evaluation led to some organisations to go for objective evaluation by developing a technique known as BARS around 1960s. It is an approach that has received greater attention in recent years. It combines major elements of the 'critical incident' and 'graphic ratings scale' approaches. The appraiser rates an employee on specific job behaviours derived from 'specific performance dimensions' (on a given job rather than on general descriptions or traits). Developing a BARS typically involves the following five steps.

1. **Generating Critical Incidents:** Critical incidents are those which are essential for the performance of the job effectively. Persons who are knowledgeable of the job in question are asked to describe specific critical incidents of effective and ineffective performance.
2. **Developing Performance Dimensions:** The critical incidents are then clustered into a smaller set of performance dimensions, usually five to ten. Each cluster, or say, dimensions are then defined.
3. **Reallocation Incidents:** Various critical incidents are reallocated dimensions by another group of people who also know the job in question. Various critical incidents so reallocated to original dimensions are clustered into various categories, with each cluster showing similar critical incidents. Those critical incidents are retained, which meet 50 to 80 percent of agreement with the cluster as classified in step 2.
4. **Scaling Incidents:** The same second group as in step 2, rates the behaviour described in each nine points scale.

Then, average effectiveness ratings for each incident are determined to decide which incidents will be included in the final anchored scales.

5. **Developing Final BARS Instrument:** A subset of the incidents is used as a behavioural anchor for the final performance dimensions. Finally, a BARS instrument with vertical scales is drawn to be used for performance appraisal. BARS method of performance appraisal is considered better than the traditional ones because it provides advantages of being a more accurate gauge.

5

Compensation Management

5.1 Meaning of Compensation

Compensation management, also known as wage and salary administration, remuneration management, or reward management, is concerned with designing and implementing the total compensation package. The traditional concept of wage and salary administration emphasized on only determination of wage and salary structures in organizational settings.

However, over the passage of time, many more forms of compensation as discussed earlier, entered the business field which necessitated to take wage and salary administration in a comprehensive way with a suitable change in its nomenclature.

Beach has defined wage and salary administration as, "wage and salary administration refers to the establishment and implementation of sound policies and practices of employee compensation. It includes such areas as job evaluation, surveys of wages and salaries, analysis of relevant organisational problems, development and maintenance of wage structure, establishing rules for administering wages, wage payments, incentives, profit sharing, wage changes and adjustments, supplementary payments, control of compensation costs and other related items".

5.2 Concept of Compensation

The literal meaning of compensation is to counter balance. In the case of human resources management, compensation is referred to as money and other benefits received by an employee for providing services to his employer. Money and benefits received may be in different forms—base compensation in money form and various benefits, which may be associated with employee's service to the employer like provident fund, gratuity, insurance scheme and any other payment which the employee receives or benefits from in lieu of such payment. Cascio has defined compensation as, "compensation includes direct cash payments, indirect payments in the form of employee benefits and incentives to motivate employees to strive for higher levels of productivity".

Based on above description of compensation, we may identify its various components as follows:

1. **Wage and Salary:** Wage and salary are the most important components of compensation and these are essential irrespective of the type of organisation. Wage is referred to as remuneration to workers particularly, hourly-rated payment. Salary refers to as remuneration paid to white-collar employees, including managerial personnel. Wages and salary are paid on the basis of fixed period of time and are normally not associated with the productivity of an employee at a particular time.
2. **Incentives:** Incentives are the additional payment to employees besides the payment of wages and salaries. Often, these are linked with productivity, either in terms of higher production or cost saving or both. These incentives may be given on an individual or group basis.
3. **Fringe Benefits:** Fringe benefits include such benefits provided to the employees having a long-term impact like provident fund, gratuity, pension; or occurrence of certain events like medical benefits, accident relief, health and life insurance; or facilitation in performance of job like uniforms, canteens, recreation, etc.
4. **Perquisites:** These are normally provided to managerial personnel either to facilitate their job performance or to retain them in the organisation. Such perquisites include company car, club membership, free residential accommodation, paid holiday trips, stock options, etc.

5.3 Objectives of Compensation Management

The basic objective of compensation management can be

briefly termed as meeting the needs of both employees and the organisation. Since both these needs emerge from different sources, often, there is a conflict between the two. This conflict can be understood by agency theory which explains relationship between employees and employers. The theory suggests that employers and employees are two main stakeholders in a business unit, the former assuming the role of principals and the latter assuming the role of agents. The compensation paid to employees is agency consideration. Each party to agency tries to fix this consideration in its own favour. The employers want to pay as little as possible to keep their costs low. Employees want to get as high as possible. The compensation management tries to strike a balance between these two with following specific objectives.

5.3.1 Attracting and Retaining Personnel: From 'point of view, the compensation management aims at attracting and retaining right personnel in the organisation. In the Indian corporate scene, there is no dearth of personnel at operative levels but the problems come at the managerial and technical levels, particularly for growing companies. Not only they require people who are well qualified but they are also retained in the organisation. In the present day context, managerial turnover is a big problem particularly in high knowledge-based organisations.

5.3.2 Motivating Personnel: Compensation management aims at motivating personnel for higher productivity. Monetary compensation has its own limitations in motivating people for superior performance. Alfie Kohn has gone to the extent of arguing that corporate incentive plans not only fail to work as intended but also undermine the objectives they intend to achieve. He argues that this is due to inadequate psychological assumptions on which reward systems are based. His conclusions are as follows:

- Rewards punish people—their use confirms that someone else is in control of the employee.
- Rewards rupture relationships—they create competition

where teamwork and collaboration is desired.

- Rewards ignore reasons—they relieve managers from the urgent need to explore why an employee is effective or ineffective.
- Rewards discourage risk taking—employees tend to do exactly what is required to earn the reward, and not any more.
- Rewards undermine interest—they distract both manager and the employee from consideration of intrinsic motivation.
- Notwithstanding these arguments, compensation management can be designed to motivate people through monetary compensation to some extent.

5.3.3 Optimising Cost of Compensation: Compensation management aims at optimising cost of compensation by establishing some kind of linkage with performance and compensation. It is not necessary that higher level of wages and salaries will bring higher performance automatically but depends on the kind of linkage that is established between performance and wages and salaries. Compensation management tries to attempt at this.

5.3.4 Consistency in Compensation: Compensation management tries to achieve consistency—both internal and external—in compensating employees. Internal consistency involves payment on the basis of criticality of jobs and employees' performance on jobs. Thus, higher compensation is attached to higher-level jobs.

Similarly, higher compensation is attached to higher performers in the same job. Level of jobs within an organisation is determined by job evaluation which will be discussed little later in this chapter. External consistency involves similar compensation for a job in all organisations. Though there are many factors involved in the determination of wage and salary structure for a job in an organisation which may result into some kind of disparity in the compensation of a particular job as compared to other organisations, compensation management tries to reduce this disparity.

5.4 Compensation Management Process

In order to achieve the objectives of compensation management, it should proceed as a process. This process has various sequential steps as discussed below.

5.4.1 Organisation's Strategy: Organisation's overall strategy—though not a step of compensation management—is the starting point in the total human resource management process including compensation management. Companies operating in different types of market/product having varying level of maturity, adopt different strategies and matching compensation strategy and blend of different compensation methods. Thus, it can be seen that organisations follow different strategies in different market situations and align their compensation strategy and contents with these strategies. In a growing market, an organisation can expand its business through internal expansion or takeover and merger of other organisations in the same line of business or a combination of both. In such a growing market, the inputs, particularly human resources, do not grow in the same proportion as the business expands.

Therefore, in order to make the growth strategy successful, the organisation has to pay high cash to attract talents. For example, information technology is a fast growing business presently and we find maximum mergers and higher managerial compensation in this industry. In a mature market, the organisation does not grow through additional investment but stabilises and the growth comes through making the present investment more effective, known as learning curve growth. In such a situation, average cash and moderate incentives may work. The benefits which have been standardised have to be maintained. In a declining market, the organisation has to harvest profit through cash generation and cost cutting and if this cannot be sustained over the long run, the possible retrenchment of business to invest somewhere else. In such a case, compensation strategy involves cost control with below average cash and incentive payments.

Cascio has observed that in viewing the compensation from strategic point of view, the companies do the following:

- They recognise remuneration as a pivotal control and incentive mechanism that can be used flexibly by the management to attain business objectives.
- They make the pay system an integral part of strategy formulation.
- They integrate pay considerations into strategic decision-making processes, such as those that involve planning and control.
- They view the company's performance as the ultimate criterion of the success of the strategic pay decisions and operational remuneration programmes.

5.4.2 Compensation Policy: Compensation policy is derived from organisational strategy and its policy on overall human resource management. In order to make compensation management to work effectively, the organisation should clearly specify its compensation policy, which must include the basis for determining base compensation, incentives and benefits and various types of perquisites to various levels of employees. The policy should be linked with the organisational philosophy on human resources and strategy. Besides, many external factors which impinge on the policy must also be taken care, like job analysis and evaluation. Job analysis provides basis for defining job description and job specification, with the former dealing with various characteristics and responsibilities involved in a job and the latter dealing with qualities and skills required in job performance. Job analysis also provides base for job evaluation which determines the relative worth of various jobs in the organisation. The relative worth of various jobs determines the compensation package attached with each job.

5.4.3 Analysis of Contingent Factors: Compensation plan is always formulated in the light of various factors, both external and internal, which affect the operation of human resource management system. Various external factors are conditions of human resource market, cost of living, level of economic development, social factors, pressure of trade unions and various labour laws dealing with compensation management. Various internal factors are organisation's ability to pay and employees' related factors such as work performance, seniority, skills, etc. These factors may be analysed through wage/salary survey. The impact of these factors will be discussed later.

5.4.4 Design and Implementation of Compensation Plan: After going through the above steps, the organisation may be able to design its compensation plan incorporating base compensation with provision of wage/salary increase over a period of time, various incentive plans and benefits and perquisites. Sometimes, these are determined by external party, for example, pay commissions for government employees as well as for public sector enterprises. After designing the compensation plan, it is implemented. Implementation of compensation plan requires its communication to employees and putting this into practice.

5.4.5 Evaluation and Review: A compensation plan is not a rigid and fixed one but a dynamic once, since it is affected by a variety of factors which are dynamic. Therefore, compensation management should have a provision for evaluating and reviewing the compensation plan. After implementation of the plan, it will generate results either in terms of intervening variables like employee satisfaction and morale or in terms of end-result variable like increase in productivity. However, this latter variable is more important. The evaluation of compensation plan must be done in this light. If it does not work as intended, there should be review of the plan, necessitating a fresh look.

5.5 Types of Compensation

1. Primary compensation.
2. Incentive compensation.

5.5.1 Primary Compensation: It is basic pay in the form of wages or salaries. The word wage is used to denote payment to hourly rated production workers and word salary is used to denote payments to clerical, supervisory and managerial employees.

A. Time as a Basis for Pay: The oldest and most common system of paying employees is on the basis of time, rate per hour, per day, per week, per month or per year.

The merits of the system are as under:

1. It is simple to understand.
2. It is liked by trade unions because it assures a guaranteed income for a given period of work.
3. It helps in maintaining the quality of output.
4. It saves machine from being overworked and damaged.
5. It protects employees from overwork and fatigue.
6. It is the only satisfactory system when the output is not distinguishable or measurable.

Following are the demerits of this system.

1. This system does not distinguish between efficient and inefficient workers. All workers are paid equal remuneration irrespective of their quantity of output. Hence, the more efficient among them either reduce their speed and efficiency or leave the organization.
2. In order to make the labourers work without wasting their time, supervision becomes necessary. This increases the cost of production.

B. Nominal and Real Wages: Wages can be expressed in two ways. When they are expressed in terms of money paid to the worker they are called nominal wages. But when they are expressed in terms of their purchasing power with reference to some base year, they are called real wages. These wages are arrived at by making adjustment in the nominal wages for the rise or fall in the cost of living.

How do we measure changes in the cost of living, or changes in the prices that consumers pay? The measuring rod is the consumer price index number. This index number is intended to show over a period of time the average percentage change in the prices paid by the consumers belonging to the population group proposed to be covered by the index for a fixed list of goods and services consumed by them. The average percentage change, measured by the index, is calculated month after month with reference to a fixed period. This fixed period is known as the 'base period of the index; and since the object of the index is to measure the effect of price changes only, the price changes have to be determined with reference to a fixed list of goods and services of consumption which is known as a fixed basket of goods and services.

C. How are Wages Determined? Economists have developed a number of theories which try to explain how wages are determined on a macro level. The subsistence theory of wages, for example, states that the real wages of unskilled workers always remain at or very little above subsistence level. If real wages rise more than enough to provide a bare subsistence, the population would expand at a greater rate than the increase of food and other necessities. The growth of population would increase the number of workers seeking jobs and the pressure of the big supply of labour would force wages down again to subsistence level. Thus, improvement in real wages can only be temporary. This theory has considerable validity in a heavily populated country with high birth rate like India. The wages of the great majority of workers in our country are still on the subsistence level and may continue to be so until our development programmes cause our rate of productivity growth to become considerably greater than the rate of population growth.

According to the marginal productivity theory of wages, in every enterprise there is a point beyond which it will not pay the management to engage more labourers. At this point, the labourer produces just enough to cover his cost towards the employer. All the labourers being assumed to be of the same quality, they will all receive the same wages, i.e., the wages representing the product of the marginal labourer. This is also not correct. In actual practice, wages of labourers, even if they are of the same quality, differ.

What then determines the wages of a worker? In actual practice, it seems to be determined by a number of factors such as the philosophy of management towards wages, region-cum-industry settlements, internal pricing through job evaluation, employer's capacity to pay, court judgements, local area going rates, collective bargaining and government laws.

D. Factors Affecting Wages: On the basis of above discussion, we may summarise the factors affecting wage rates as under:

1. **Demand for and Supply of Labour:** Demand and supply conditions of labour have considerable influence on the determination of wage rates. If there is a short supply of labour, the wages may be high whereas if there is no dearth of labour, the wages tend to be low.
2. **Labour Unions:** If the labourers are well organized into strong trade unions, their bargaining power would be high and they can demand higher rates of wages. On the other hand, if the labourers are not organized, the management may fix low wages.
3. **Cost of Living:** The cost of living of workers also has a strong influence on the rate of wages. If this factor is not considered, the labourers may not be in a position to make both ends meet and this will affect their efficiency. Hence, progressive employers consider this factor also.
4. **Prevailing Wage Rates:** Prevailing wages in a particular industry are also taken into account by the employers while deciding wage levels for their employees. By considering the prevailing wage level, employers will come reasonable close to the wage level of competitors, and this will enable them to retain and attract qualified workers to the organizations.
5. **Ability to Pay:** The wage level, to a large extent, is determined by the ability of the enterprise to pay its workers. The ability to pay in turn is determined by the profit-earning capacity of the enterprise.
6. **Job Requirements:** Job requirements is also an important factor affecting wages. Jobs requiring specialized knowledge or involving much mental or manual effort are

priced higher than those which are light or which do not need any specialized knowledge.

7. **State Regulation:** State regulation is another important factor influencing wage rates. As the state assumes responsibility for safeguarding the interest of citizens, it has to step in to regulate the wage rates of labourers through legislative measures.
8. **Increment System:** In some organizations, wages automatically increase annually at a prescribed rate without any relation to workers' performance. In some other organizations, annual increases are based on merit. Thus, the prevailing system of granting increments also affects wages.

5.5.2 Incentives: These are all plans that provide extra pay for extra performance, in addition to the regular job. They maintain and create sound industrial relations and also improve the quality of the employees.

6

Wages and Fringe Benefits

The wage structure decision has to do with determining the wage rates for jobs. It combines the external marketplace considered in the pay level decision with the relative value that different jobs have in the organization. The organizational value of a job is determined through job evaluation, which in turn relies on job analysis to provide the information required for the evaluation. The organizational and market values of jobs are integrated through the development of a wage structure, which defines job levels or grades, and assigns wage rates to those grades by reference to market rates.

6.1 Wages

In most organizations, wage and salary rates are still assigned to jobs. The relationships between the pay for jobs involve pay structure decisions. Although organizations often make pay level decisions (how much to pay) and pay structure decisions (pay relationship) at the same time, these decisions and the process by which they are reached require separate treatment. Actually, wage structures represent wage relationships of all kinds. Analysis of wage differentials of any kind (geographic, industry, community, or occupation) deals with wage structure issues. But because our primary focus is on pay decisions in organizations, our concern is with pay differences between jobs. In fact, determining the pay structure of an organization may be usefully described as putting dollar signs on jobs. Decisions on wage relationships among jobs within an organization are largely within the control of its decision makers. Wage level decisions are usually influenced more by forces external to the organization than are wage structure decisions.

Some organizations pay for skills possessed by employees

rather than for the jobs employees hold. The rationale is usually serious and continual due to skill shortages experienced by the organization. But most organizations measure employee contributions first in terms of the jobs employees hold. One interesting analysis of organizational compensation decisions is that pay structure decisions are intended to achieve retention of employees through prevention of dissatisfaction and encouragement of employee cooperation. Pay level decisions, in this analysis, are intended to attract employees. To this analysis, could be added the statement that wage structure decisions are intended to encourage employees to make a career with the organization and to accept training in preparation for higher-level jobs.

6.1.1 Determinants of the Wage Structure

A. Economic Determinants: Adam Smith explains occupational wage differentials in terms of: (i) hardship, (ii) difficulty of learning the job, (iii) stability of employment, (iv) responsibility of the job, and (v) chance for success or failure in the work. This is a theory of wage structure. But his standards of worth are equally useful in explaining the complexity of wage structure decisions. The market value of an item is the price it brings in a market where demand and supply are equal. Use value is the value an individual buyer or seller anticipates through use of the item. Use value obviously varies among individuals and over time.

- **Job Worth:** These two concepts of worth and the concept of internal labour markets combine to explain important differences among employers in wage structure decisions. Organizations with relatively open internal labour markets (organizations in which most jobs are filled from outside) make much use of market value. They also make much use of wage and salary surveys in wage structure decisions. Conversely, organizations with relatively closed internal labour markets (most jobs are filled from inside) emphasize use value. Their analysis of job worth relies more heavily on perceptions of organization members of the relative value of jobs.

- **Training:** Some other wage structure determinants derived from economic analysis may be noted. Training requirements of jobs in terms of length, difficulty, and whether the training is provided by society, employers, or individuals constitute a primary factor in human-capital analysis and thus job worth. The interaction of ability requirements with training requirements can yield different job values, depending on the scarcity of the ability required and the number of people who try to make it in the occupation and fail.
- **Employees' Tastes:** Employee tastes and preferences are another economic factor. People differ in the occupations they like and dislike. In like manner, occupations have non-monetary advantages and disadvantages of many kinds. Worker expectations of future earnings strongly influence occupational choice and thus labour supplies. Unfortunately, labour-market information is far from perfect, and responses to labour-market shortages are likely to be more prompt than responses to oversupplies.
- **Trade Unions:** Industrial as opposed to craft unionism has also been shown by economic analysis to affect wage structures. Industrial unions, with their heavy proportions of semi-skilled members, are more likely to favour absolute increases. Although large organizations where employees are represented by industrial unions may have a highly differentiated wage structure, they pay less attention to percentage differentials than they would in the presence of craft unions.
- **Discrimination:** Another economic determinant is discrimination. Although wage differentials based on sex or race are unlawful, they still exist. The extent to which such differences are based on productivity differences or represent discrimination is very much a wage structure issue.

B. Social Determinants: Just-price theory advocated setting wages in accordance with the pre-established status distribution—wages were to be systematically regulated to keep each class in its customary place in society. The theory emphasized equity, the tying of wages to status, and the preservation of customary relationships. But whereas social forces generally operate to maintain what is customary and accepted, market forces have been operating to narrow differentials. Market forces usually operate through the shifting of labour supplies. One reason that social forces seem to predominate is the slow reaction of supply to price. Supply shortages are more effective in raising pay than supply surpluses are in lowering it.

C. Organizational Determinants: Organizations develop jobs to get their work done. Labour services acquire specific economic meaning only in relation to the particular jobs in which they are performed. In our economic system, the organization typically designs jobs and selects employees to fill them. The jobs the organization designs are the source of the contributions provided by employees and a primary determinant of their rewards. Through these jobs and pay decisions about them, the organization is structuring the market for labour services. Other organizations differing in technology, management competence, competitive economics, and collective bargaining are also designing jobs. As a consequence, it is quite unlikely that the jobs designed by one organization will be identical to those of other organizations. Furthermore, the decisions that go into job design are not made once and for all, but are subject to revision, as market conditions, technology, and institutional influences change.

6.2 Fringe Benefits

Benefits given to employees in addition to their salary or wage are called 'fringe benefits'. Thus, fringe benefits are those monetary and non-monetary benefits given to the employees during and post-employment period which are connected with employment but not to the employees' contribution to the organization. Cockmar defined it as those benefits which are not provided by an employer to or for the benefit of employees and which are not in the form of wages, salaries and time related payments.

The fringe benefits cover bonus, social security measures, retirement benefits like provident fund, gratuity, pension workmen's compensation, housing, medical, canteen, co-operative credit, consumer stores, educational facilities, recreational facilities, financial advice and so on.

6.2.1 Objectives: These are as under:

1. To create and improve sound industrial relations.
2. To boost up employee morale.
3. To motivate the employees by identifying and satisfying their unsatisfied needs.
4. To provide qualitative work environment and work life.
5. To provide security to the employees against social risk like old age benefit and maternity benefits.
6. To protect the health of the employees and to provide safety to the employees against accidents.
7. To promote employees' welfare by providing welfare measures like recreation facilities.
8. To create sense of belongingness among employees
9. To meet requirements of various legislations relating to fringe benefits.

6.2.2 Factors Influencing Employee Benefit:

1. Absolute and per capita cost of fringe benefit.
2. Organization's financial ability to provide the benefits.
3. Employee's deficiencies or needs.
4. The bargaining strength of trade unions.
5. Employee's significance to the organization.
6. Fax benefits to the organization and individual employees.
7. Need for building public image for the organization.
8. Organization's awareness and policy towards social responsibility.
9. Employee's reactions to the benefits.

6.2.3 Types of Fringe Benefits:

A. Employment Security: Benefits under this head

include employment insurance, technological adjustment pay, leave travel pay, overtime pay, level for negotiation, leave for maternity, leave for grievances, holidays, cost of living bonus, call back pay, lay off pay, retiring rooms, jobs to the sons/daughter of the employees.

B. Health Protection: Benefits include accident insurance, disability insurance, health insurance, hospitalization, life insurance, medical care, sick benefits, sick leave.

C. Old Age and Retirement Benefits: It include deferred income plan pension, gratuity, provident fund, old age pension, old age counselling, medical benefits for retired employees, travelling concession to retired employees.

D. Personnel Identification, Participation and Stimulation: The category covers the following benefits: anniversary awards, attendance bonus, canteen, cooperative credit societies, educational facilities, beauty parlour services, housing, income tax aid, counselling, quality bonus, recreational programmes, stress counselling, safety measures etc.

In addition to fringe benefits, managements provide different types of non-monetary rewards also. These non-monetary rewards include:

1. Treats covering free lunches, festival bashes, coffee breaks, picnics, dinner with the boss, dinner for the family, birthday treats.
2. Knick-knacks covering desk accessories, company watches, tie-pins, brooches, diaries/planners, calendars, wallets and T-shirts.
3. Awards including trophies, plaques, citations, certificates, scrolls, letters of appreciation.
4. Social acknowledgment including informal recognition, recognition at office get together, socialisation of advice, suggestions etc.
5. Office environment covering redecoration, flexible hours etc.
6. Tokens covering movie tickets, vacation trips, early time-offs etc.
7. On-the-job rewards including increased responsibility, job

rotation, training etc.

6.2.4 Advantages of Fringe Benefits: Advantages of non-monetary rewards include:

1. Non-monetary rewards motivate employees to perform better.
2. Non-monetary rewards build employee self-esteem.
3. Employees become more loyal to the company.
4. These benefits create an atmosphere where change is not resented.
5. These benefits can be provided without any extra cost.
6. Create close bondage between the company and employee family.

6.2.5 Disadvantages of Fringe Benefits: The non-monetary rewards, despite the advantages discussed above, suffer from the following disadvantages.

1. These benefits demotivate the employees, if the processes are not transparent.
2. These rewards may result in short-sighted and hasty decision-making.
3. These rewards may result in unhealthy competition among employees.
4. Work intrudes on the home life of employees.
5. Employees feel that managements concentrate on the non-cost programmes.
6. These rewards will not work, if monetary rewards are not adequate.

7

Placement, Induction, Transfer and Promotion

7.1 Placement

Placement in simple words, means sending the newly employed person to one or the other department for work. Placement should be based on the qualifications and qualities of the person selected. It should also be based on the staff requirements of different departments. It is the duty of the personnel department to send the new employee to a suitable department. In addition, he should be introduced properly to the head of that department. The placement arrangement should be ready before the joining date of the newly selected person. The placement in the initial period may be temporary as changes are likely after the completion of training. The employee may be later transferred to the job where he can do better justice.

7.2 Induction

7.2.1 Orientation or Preliminary Training: Induction is the welcoming process to make the new employee feel at home and generate in him a feeling of belongingness for the organisation. It is concerned with the problem of introducing or orienting a new employee to his work group—supervisor and the integration and agreement between the organisation's goals and the personal goals of the new employee. After selecting compatible personnel, the organisation must communicate to the new employees its philosophies, policies, customs and practices. Planned induction welcomes the new employee, creates a good attitude, reduces labour turnover and the employee feels at home right from the beginning.

Induction may also be viewed as the socialising process by which the organisation seeks to make an individual its agent for the achievement of its objectives and the individual seeks to make an agency of the organisation for the achievement of his personal goals.

A. Purpose: An induction or introduction programme should try to achieve the following objectives:

1. To build up the new employee's confidence in the organisation and in himself so that he may become an efficient employee.
2. To promote a feeling of belonging and loyalty to the organisation among new comers.
3. To ensure that the new employee may not form false impression regarding the new place of work because first impression is the last impression.
4. To give the new entrant the information he needs such as location of locker room, cafeteria and other facilities, time to break off, leave rules etc.
5. To foster a close relationship between the new workers and the old workers and supervisors.

B. Contents: The induction programme is generally informal in case of small firms. It may be formal of the duration of two to four weeks, in case of big organisations. Orientation and training course should broadly cover the following:

1. Company's history and philosophy.
2. Products of the company.
3. Company's organisation structure.
4. Location of departments and employee services.
5. Personnel policies and practices.
6. Employees' activities.
7. Grievance procedure.
8. Rules and regulations.
9. Safety measures.
10. Standing orders.

7.3 Transfer

Transfers of employees are quite common in all

organizations. A transfer may be defined as a change in job within the organization where the new job is substantially equal to the old in terms of pay, status and responsibilities. Transfers are possible from one department to the other or from one plant to the other.

Transfers may be initiated by the organization or by the employees with the approval of the organization. Transfers have a number of objectives such as moving employees to positions with a higher priority in terms of organization goals, placing employees in positions more appropriate to their interests or abilities and filling department vacancies with employees from overstaffed departments.

Transfers may be resorted to due to changes in organizational structure or changes in the volume of work. Transfers may become necessary in an organization for a variety of other reasons also. Management may think it necessary to rectify the mistakes in the selection and placement of employees.

7.3.1 Transfer versus Promotion: The term 'transfer' refers to changes in which the pay status and job conditions of new position or job are almost the same as that of the old. In case of promotion, the new position has higher pay status and job conditions as compared with the old one. A transfer may be associated with a higher pay. But it is counter balanced by changes in other conditions.

Promotion implies an upward elevation of an individual in terms of job responsibilities, pay scale and status. It represents an advancement and going up a step in the career ladder. It is a case of upward mobility which most of the employees seek for their career advancement. But transfer refers to a lateral shift of an individual from one job position to another on the same occupational level and pay scale.

Promotion represents a recognition of and reward for merit, good performance and behaviour and so on. It tends to improve satisfaction of the person promoted and to induce him to perform better. Transfer does not have these implications. Considerations of merit and seniority do not generally enter into transfer matters; there may however be some instances where an employee with good performance is transferred to another unit to utilize his skills more meaningfully. The incentive value of transfers is generally low unless the new job position has more powers.

7.3.2 Types of Transfers: Most organizations generally resort to three types of transfers which are discussed below.

A. Remedial Transfers: As the name suggests, these transfers are made to rectify the situation caused by faculty selection and placement procedures. For instance, if the initial placement of an individual is faulty or he cannot adjust to a job, his transfer to a more appropriate job is desirable. This will act as a follow up measure of selection and placement procedures and will help the employees to adjust themselves to suitable jobs.

B. Versatility Transfers: Such transfers are made to increase versatility of the employees from one job to another and one department to another. Transfers or job rotations are used as a devise to train the employees. The employee is provided a varied and broader job experience by moving from one job to another. Such transfers help the employees to get prepared for further promotions.

C. Production Transfers: Such transfers are resorted to when there is a need of manpower in one department and surplus manpower exists in the other. Thus, production transfers are made from a department which is overstaffed to the other department where manpower needs have increased or vacancies have occurred through separations. They prevent layoffs from the overstaffed departments. It is not a good policy to have in the same organization, layoffs in one department and employees being recruited in another department for the similar types of job.

7.3.3 Rationale of Transfer: The need for transfer may arise due to any one or more of the following reasons:

1. There may be a variation in the volume of work in different departments or sections.

2. An employee may not do justice to a job. He may be transferred to another job to utilize his services properly or to allow him to adjust in the organization properly.
3. In many organizations, transfers are made as a matter of policy after an employee has stayed on a job for a particular period. This serves as a basis of training by rotation from one job to another.
4. Transfer may be requested by an employee on health grounds, family circumstances or some other personnel problem.

7.3.4 Transfer Policy: Whatever may be the reason of a transfer, it should be resorted to as a part of an overall personnel policy and not for the sake of transfer only. Transfers should not be made frequently or without any reason because when an employee is transferred from one department to another or from one job to another, he is bound to be unsettled for sometime. He will take time to get accustomed to his new assignment and environment. Thus, performance is bound to suffer for sometime. It would be better if the transfer is made in consultation with the employee concerned and is for the similar job or for which he has got some aptitude or training. The transfer scheme should be understood by all the employees and there should be no ad hoc transfers for the reasons described above. Sometimes, transfers by rotation may be adopted as a part of personnel policy to provide training opportunities to the employees for gaining experience in as many departments and types of work as possible.

A systematic transfer policy must be evolved by the personnel department as a part of the overall personnel programme. It must be put in writing and should meet the following requirements:

1. Transfer policy should specify clearly the types and circumstances under which transfers will be used.
2. It should lay down the basis for transfers. For instance, where two persons desire transfer for the same job, would seniority or merit or any other factor be the deciding factor?

3. It should indicate the executives responsible for initiating and approving the transfers.
4. It should prescribe whether the transfers can be made only within a department or also between different departments.
5. It should prescribe whether when an employee is transferred, his previous seniority credit would be retained. This is very important to avoid confusion that might arise when some employees are transferred.

7.4 Promotion

Employees are given promotions to higher posts and positions as and when vacancies are available or when new posts are created at the higher levels. Promotions are quite common in all types of employment. Promotion is treated as a better policy as compared to direct recruitment at the higher level posts. Even in government departments, promotions are common in the case of banks, insurance companies and other establishments.

Promotion means giving higher position to an employee which carries higher status, more responsibilities and higher salary. Higher status and salary are the two important features of promotion—a vacancy which in general is worth more to the organization than the incumbent's present position. In other words, promotion means advancement of an employee to a higher post with greater responsibilities and higher salary, better service conditions and thus higher status.

7.4.1 Upgradation: When the scale of salary of an employee is increased without corresponding change in job, it is called upgrading. The job itself may be upgraded to a higher scale of pay or if there variable scales of pay for the same job according to the skills required, upgrading may mean moving to a higher scale without changing the job. But promotion involves a change in salary grade of job and status. Both promotion and upgradation are devices used by management to reward employees for better performance and to increase their morale. They generate in the employee, a sense of loyalty for the organisation and stimulate him for greater effect to get further promotions.

7.4.2 Promotion versus Recruitment from Outside: Promotion may be used as a means of filling up vacancies in higher or senior positions, whenever, a higher post falls vacant. Sound personnel policy requires that it should be filled in by promotion from within the organisation if a person required possesses the skills, ability and calibre. If all such vacancies are filled up from outside, there will be no inducement for the existing staff to improve their efficiency. Absence of such prospects is apt to make the employees dissatisfied, demoralised and frustrated. This will be reflected in low quality of output, wastages, absenteeism, indiscipline and turnover of employees. The morals of the workers will also be low and it will tell upon the working of the entire enterprise.

Promotion from within to fill up the senior posts shall have the following advantages:

1. Insiders are intimately connected with the organisation structure, production process, products and different problems and they can handle the new jobs easily.
2. It will keep the morale of the employees high.
3. It will ensure sincere effort on the part of employees because they know that they may rise to senior positions by promotions.
4. The costs of training the insiders on the senior posts will be less.

7.4.3 Promotion Policy: The promotion policy must be flexible. It should not bar the outsiders who may bring valuable ideas and may be more suitable to handle the jobs than the insiders. However, discards from other organizations should always be avoided ordinarily. The demands made upon by the outside labour market should be for the beginners only unless some specially qualified outsiders fit better than any of the insider. Sound personnel policy demands that internal staff should be given a fair chance of promotion before posts are filled through outside recruitment.

The promotion policy must consider the merit, potential and seniority of the employees. The merit factors require a good procedure for evaluating the performance of the employees. The performance of each employee should be measured periodically and should form a part of the personnel records. The evaluation of performance should cover such factors as output, cooperation, initiative, willingness to accept responsibility and degree of reliability and dependability. This process has been discussed in details in the earlier chapter on 'Performance Appraisal Techniques'. The potential of the employee also depends upon his merit and ability.

Unlike merit and potentiality, seniority can be measured easily. Seniority means length of service of an employee on a particular job. Seniority generally begins to accumulate as soon as an employee is hired. Abnormal interruptions to service due to long illness or any other reasons are deducted from the total period of service. All the organizations usually follow this practice. But for bringing definiteness in the promotion policy, it must be in writing and should lay down the factors on which merit potential and seniority will be based.

Following benefits may be achieved from effective promotion policy:

1. It provides an incentive to the people in an organization to work more efficiently as it gives recognition to an employee who has done his job well.
2. It increases job satisfaction of the employees.
3. It helps keep an efficient force of employees and also attract efficient people to the organization.
4. It develops employees locally by assuring them promotion within the organization, if found fit.
5. It increases the effectiveness of the organisation.

7.4.4 Criteria of Promotion Seniority versus Merit: What should be the criteria of promotion seniority or ability? The promotion policy may be based on seniority or ability, or combination of both. If it is adopted on this basis, the promotion will be done as a matter of routine and every employee will know his place in the promotion list. There will be no chance of favoritism or dispute regarding promotion and employee morale will not be affected. It will also increase the efficacy of the employees.

Promotion on the basis of seniority has certain disadvantages also. The beginner will have no incentive to improve his performance because he knows that there is no chance of his promotion until all those senior to him, leave the organization or are promoted. This will hamper the development of those who have an aptitude to improve their performance faster because they will feel that whatever may be their performance, it will neither reduce the chances of their promotion in the due course nor help them in securing earlier than due. Because of these drawbacks, managements prefer ability as the basis of promotion.

The policy of promotion on the basis of merit has the following advantages:

1. Promotion on the basis of merit motivates the employees having potential for development.
2. Merit on the basis of promotion ensures that efficiency of the organisation is maintained.
3. Merit based promotion policy attracts young and promising candidates to apply for jobs in the organization. This in turn infuses fresh blood into the organization.

The merit of the employees may be judged either by written or oral examinations, personal interviews and their records of performance. The ability criteria, ignores the value of experience. Moreover, since there is no fool proof method of judging the ability of an employee, it is likely to lead to faulty judgment. The judgment varies from individual to individual. An employee may be considered able and fit for promotion by one superior but not by the other. It may lead to abuse of power and favoritism on the part of management. This will result in unhealthy employer-employee relationship. A sound promotion policy should be based on both the consideration, i.e. seniority and ability. It should primarily be based on the merit of the employee giving due weightage to seniority.

7.4.5 Open versus Closed Promotional System: An organization may adopt an open or a closed promotional system or a combination of both. An organization is said to have an open promotion system where it is willing to consider all its employees as potential candidates and also announce the various position openings. But where an organization does not announce the vacancies or where the candidacy is restricted and is not open for all the employees in the organization, it is said to follow a closed promotional system. Generally, the organizations use a combination of both these systems. For instance, for openings below a certain managerial lever, an organization may adopt an open promotion system and give every interested employee a chance, but for level above that, particularly managerial level, the selection may be done in a more secret fashion.

7.4.6 Demotion: Demotion is just the opposite of promotion. It is a downward movement of an employee in the organizational hierarchy with lower status and lower salary. It is a downgrading process and is insulting to an employee. Demotion is a punishment for incompetence or mistakes of serious type of penalty or punishment and should be given rarely only under exceptional circumstances and also tactfully. Demotion may be necessary in the following situations.

1. When the company curtails some of its activities—officers occupying certain posts are demoted.
2. Errors in the promotion already given are corrected through demotion.
3. It may be necessary to use demotion as a tool of disciplinary action against erring employees.

The tool of demotion should be used only when it is absolutely necessary. However, there should not be any injustice to any employee in this regard. Demotions should be made for genuine reasons. Promotions are easily accepted by employees, but demotions are not accepted easily as they affect the status, career and position of the employees. Demotion is usually treated as an insult and naturally resented by the employees in one way or the other. It is, therefore, desirable to avoid demotions as far as possible. Demotions should be an exception and not a normal rule.

8

Resignation, Layoff, Dismissal, Retirement

Separation of an employee from the organization occurs when the service agreement with the organization comes to an end because of one reason or the other. Separations arise from resignation, layoff, dismissal or retirement.

8.1 Resignation

When a separation is initiated by the employee himself, it is termed as resignation. Although some resignations may permit an organization to rectify mistakes in procurement of personnel or to bring new blood into the affected unit, but excessive turnover may prove costly to the organization. There are resignations which are unavoidable and the organization should investigate the real causes of such resignations and try to escape avoidable resignations because these indicate for an improvement in the organizational selection and training of the employees.

Sometimes there are unavoidable resignations such as those for reasons of marriage (frequent in case of girls) or for entering a different career. In any case, it is better to conduct 'exit interview' to obtain data for analyzing causes of turnover. Such interviews may be conducted by a responsible person from the personnel department. There interviews also serve some additional purposes, such as making sure that the employee leaving the organization, has fully handed over the charge to somebody else and that the employee understands the disposition of his various benefit programmes.

8.2 Layoff

The purpose of layoff is to reduce the financial burden on the organization in the event that resources cannot be utilized profitably. Layoff involves temporary removal from the payroll, of the people with surplus skills. According to Section 2 of the Industrial Disputes Act, 1947, layoff means failure. In a larger sense it may include, refusal or inability of an employee, shortage of power or raw materials, accumulation of excess stock, breakdown of machinery etc. Thus, the essentials of a layoff are as under.

- There must be failure or refusal or inability of the employee to continue with his employment.
- The workers laid off must be on the muster rolls of the establishment on the date of layoff.
- The reasons for layoff could be shortage of coal, raw material or power, or accumulation of stocks or break down of machines or other similar reasons.
- The emergency leading to employer's inability must be temporary.
- Employer and employee relationship does not come to an end, but is merely suspended during the period of emergency.

Thus, layoff involves a great cost to the organisation. Hence, the employer should take every step to avoid the causes of layoff. Layoff means temporary separation of the employees and it may later on lead to retrenchment of the employees. Whatever may be the case, the organisation has to suffer a great loss because it loses the benefit of all expenses incurred on selection, placement and training and consequently, compensation has also to be paid to the employees so laid off.

8.3 Dismissal

Dismissal or discharge involves separating an employee from the payroll for violation of organisational rules or for inadequate performance. Discharge is often labelled as capital punishment for the employees and so is considered a drastic step. It must, therefore, be resorted to with great care and must be supported with a just and sufficient cause. Since dismissal is a traumatic experience for everyone concerned, most managers are reluctant to undertake such action. But despite this, discharge of employees is not uncommon and managements guard their prerogative to discharge, as an indispensable tool for maintaining standards of performance. It is generally used as a last step after all attempts at salvaging the employee have failed.

An employee may be discharged on the ground of unsatisfactory performance or misconduct. Unsatisfactory performance refers to persistent failure on the part of the employee to perform his assigned work duties to meet the desired job standards. This may be due to various reasons. An employee may show an adverse attitude towards the organisation or may not take interest in his work. He may not be properly skilled or qualified to handle his job efficiently. An employee is discharged on the ground of unsatisfactory performance, when it is clear that he has no potential to further improve over the job.

Misconduct refers to wilful violation of organisational rules and regulations by the employees. It includes indiscipline, insubordination and dishonesty and hence constitutes a major cause for dismissals.

8.4 Retirement

Retirement of an employee is an important event in his life and also has an important impact on the organisation where he worked for a major portion of his life. Therefore, at the time of parting or farewell, the personnel manager should arrange a special interview with the employee. He should thank the employee for his service to the organisation and should ask him to speak about the changes or improvements he would like to be introduced in the organisation.

Retirement may be of the following kinds:

8.4.1 Compulsory Retirement: The employee must retire compulsorily after attaining a specific age in central government and state government offices. In case of private organisations, employees may be given extension until they are suitable to do the work. Managerial or technical personnel may be re-employed after the period of service if the contract of service is over.

8.4.2 Forced Retirement: If an employee is found guilty either in court of law or has violated the conditions enumerated in the service agreement, he may be forced to retire from the service with or without any benefit.

8.4.3 Premature Retirement: If an employee becomes disabled in an accident or due to some disease, he may be given the option of retiring by the management before attaining the retirement age with full benefits of retirement. There may be some other personal reasons also for premature retirement such as bad health, family problem etc.

9

Organizational Development and Change

9.1 Organizational Development

The term organizational development (OD) first appeared around 1957 when it was used by a number of theorists including Blake and Mouton, Shepard and Beckhard. It is based on behavioural sciences particularly psychology and sociology.

OD is an educational strategy which focuses on the whole culture of an organization in order to bring about planned change. It seeks to change beliefs, attitudes, values and structures that infect the entire culture of an organization so that the organization may adapt to better technology and environment with the pace of change. Thus, organization development may be defined as a technique for bringing change in the entire aspects of the organization so that change is easily absorbed.

According to Backhard, "organization development is an effort which is: (i) planned, (ii) organization wide, (iii) managed from the top, and (iv) increases organizational effectiveness and health through planned intervention in the organization processes, using behavioural sciences knowledge". The elements of this definition are examined below:

- **Planned Change:** OD is a planned evaluation and improvement. This planning includes examining the present and systematically diagnosing the organization's needs and formulating a specific plan for improvement, and mobilizing the organizational resources needed to carry out the change.
- **Organisation Wide:** The goal of OD is to improve the effectiveness of the total organization. Although specific aspects may focus on sub-systems, yet the underlying view is that an organization is a system of inter-related facts.

- **Managed from the Top:** In an OD effort, the manager is a key element to success. For the change to work well, commitment is essential at all levels. The commitment is crucial because it serves as a standard for the rest of the organization's members.

9.1.1 Need for OD: Organization development (OD) is a newly emerging discipline directed towards using behavioural science knowledge to assist organizations adjusting more rapidly to change. Using a systems approach, OD has grown rapidly in response to a need—the need for organization to remain viable and to survive in the world of change. Two important factors have caused the use of OD as a technique for planned change. Firstly, training for change does not work properly only through reward structure but is also based on the environment of the organization in which people work. Secondly, in a dynamic environment the change is extremely rapid. This requires a highly receptive and effective organization so that changes are implemented and absorbed to make an organization survive and grow. OD helps a lot in this direction. It (OD) tries to free up communication tightness by increasing the amount, trust, and candour of communication. It seeks to build problems solving capability of communication by improving group dynamics and problem confrontation. In short, it reaches into all aspects of organization culture in order to make it more humanly responsive".

9.1.2 Benefits of OD: Margulies and Raia have given the following benefits of organization development:

1. It provides opportunities for people to function as human beings rather than mere resources in the productive process.
2. It gives each member of the organization, opportunities to develop to his full potential.
3. Seeks to make the organization more effective in meeting all its goals.
4. Tries to create an environment in which exciting and challenging work can be found.

5. Gives people in an organization, the chance to influence how they relate to the organization and the work environment.
6. It treats each human being as a person with a complex set of needs, all of which are important in him or her work and life.

9.1.3 Limitations of OD: Organization development is an important technique of increasing change. It has certain limitations also which are listed below.

1. OD can be no more powerful than the behavioural science concepts on which it is based. Behavioural science has many limitations which are applicable to organizational development.
2. OD requires use of certain persons who can take initiatives to bring about the change. Complacent people cannot be helpful in implementing organizational development.
3. OD cannot be applied without giving due consideration to the local circumstances or existing considerations of the organization. The local circumstances may pose a problem in adapting to change.

9.1.4 Assumptions of OD: Organization development is based on certain assumptions which are follows:

1. Most individuals have drives towards personal growth and development. However, the work habits are a response to the work environment rather than personality traits. Accordingly, efforts to change work habits should be directed towards changing how the person is treated than towards attempting to change the person.
2. Highest productivity can be achieved when the individual goals are integrated with the organizational goals.
3. Cooperation is more effective than conflict. Conflict tends to erode trust, prohibit collaboration and eventually limit the effectiveness of the organization. In healthy organizations, efforts are made at all levels to treat conflict as a problem, subject to problem solving methods.
4. Suppression of feelings adversely affects problem solving,

personal growth and satisfaction with one's work. Accordingly, free expression of feelings is an important ingredient for commitment to work.

5. Growth of individuals is facilitated by relationships which are open, supportive and trusting. Accordingly, the level of interpersonal trust, support and cooperation should be as high as possible.

9.1.5 Steps in Organization Development: Lawrence and Lorsch have provided four steps in OD, namely diagnosis, planning action, implementing action and evaluation. These are explained below.

A. Diagnosis of Problem: OD programme starts with the identification of the problem in the organization. Analysis of various symptoms—both overt and covert—may help in identifying the problem. Diagnosis of a problem will provide its causes and determine the nature of future action needed. A lot of bad decisions are taken because the decision makers do not have a good grasp of the problem. Therefore, adequate information should be gathered to identify the real problem.

B. Planning Strategy for Change: Many firms employ management consultants to suggest strategy for change. The management consultant or OD practitioner should attempt to transform diagnosis of the problem into a proper action plan involving the overall goals for change, determination of basic approach for attaining these goals and the sequence of detailed scheme for implementing the approach.

C. Implementing the Change: Although it is quite simple to identify change after it has occurred, it is very difficult to influence the direction of change while it is underway. Planning and implementation of change are interdependent. The way in which a change is planned has an important impact on the way in which it is carried out and conversely. The problems in implementing change also have an impact on the modification of change plan. OD practitioners have an important role in implementing change.

D. Evaluation: OD is very long process. So there is a

great need for careful monitoring to get precise feedback regarding what is going on after the OD programme starts. This will help in making suitable modifications whenever necessary. For evaluation of OD programme, the use of critique sessions, appraisal of change efforts and comparison of pre- and post-training behavioural patterns are quite effective.

9.1.6 OD Intervention Techniques

A. Behavioural Techniques: These techniques are designed to affect the behaviour of individual and group. These include:

1. Sensitivity training.
2. Management by objectives.
3. Grid organization development.

B. Non-behavioural Techniques: These techniques are much more structured than the behavioural techniques. These include:

1. Change in the organization structure.
2. Work design.
3. Job enrichment.

C. Miscellaneous Techniques: In addition to above techniques, there are certain other techniques which are used in organization development, such as:

1. Survey feedback.
2. Process consultation.
3. Team building.

9.1.7 Sensitivity or T-Group Training: A manager's behaviour is not how he thinks or behaves, but how others view his behaviour. Sensitivity training has the objective of expanding a person's understanding of how his behaviour affects others and his reaction to the behaviour of others. In this approach, the participants are encouraged to undertake considerable self-examination. Sensitivity training represents a valuable psychological experience and a highly effective approach for the study of interpersonal relationships.

The T-Group training is a major category of sensitivity

training and consists of an unstructured group of about 8-10 people with no leader, no agenda and no stated goal. The group is expected to develop interactions in whatever ways its members like. The emphasis is on "here and now" and a "face-to-face" interaction. Some benefits of T-Group Training are:

1. The participants learn more about themselves, specially their own weaknesses and emotions.
2. It develops insights into how the participants react to others and how others react to them.
3. It helps to understand group processes, inter-member, interactions, interpersonal relations and how to manage people through means other than power.
4. It helps to assess one's values and goals as a result of analysis of direct experiences.

9.1.8 Grid Development: Grid organizational development is based on Blake and Mouton's model of leadership called the 'managerial grid'. Their model depicts two prevailing concerns found in all organizations—concern for productivity and concern for people. Some managers are high in concern for productivity and concern for people; others are high in concern for people but low in concern for productivity. Besides helping managers evaluate their concern for people and productivity, the managerial grid stresses the importance of developing a team-management leadership style.

In grid OD, change agents use a questionnaire to determine the existing styles of managers to help them to re-examine their own styles and work towards maximum effectiveness. A grid OD programme commonly has six phases.

A. Training: Key managers learn about grid concepts and how they are applied in a week long seminar. They assess their own managerial styles and work on improving such skills as team development, group problem solving and communications. After appropriate instructions, these key managers will work to implement the grid programme throughout the organization.

B. Team Development: The trained managers bring their new understanding of managerial grid concepts to the work situation. Emphasis is placed on improving both manager-subordinate relationships and team effectiveness.

C. Inter-group Development: This phase focuses on the relationship between the organization's work groups to improve coordination and cooperation. Inter-group conflicts are dealt with openly and joint problem solving procedures are developed.

D. Organizational Goal Setting: Top managers together create an ideal model of the organization. They set goals to be tested, evaluated and refined by managers and subordinates working together throughout the organization.

E. Goal Attainment: Organization members seek to make the ideal model a reality. Each one examines how their activities should be carried out in order to achieve excellence and they proceed to take whatever corrective actions are necessary.

F. Stabilization: Eventually, the results of all the phases are evaluated to determine which areas of the organization still need improvement or alternation. Efforts are made to stabilize positive changes and to identify new areas of opportunity for the organization.

9.1.9 Organizational Redesign: An organization's structure may be changed to make it more efficient by redefining the flow of authority. There can also be changes in functional responsibility—a move from product to matrix organizational structure.

Organizational structure often reflects the personal desires, needs and values of the chief executive. Changing structure, therefore, may create resistance and concern because people are worried about their power or status, or how the change will affect their work groups.

A. Job Enrichment: Job enrichment implies increasing the contents of a job or the deliberate upgrading of responsibility, scope and challenge in work. "Job enrichment" is a motivational technique which emphasizes the need for a challenging and interesting work. It suggests that jobs be redesigned so that intrinsic satisfaction is derived from doing the job.

The term 'job enrichment" should be distinguished from the term "job enlargement". Job enlargement attempts to make a job more varied by removing the dullness associated with performing repetitive operations. It involves a horizontal loading of expansion i.e., the addition of more tasks of the same nature.

B. Work Design: Work design is a broad term meaning the process of defining tasks and jobs to achieve both organizational and employee goals. It must, therefore, take into account the nature of the business (organizational interest), the organizational structure, the information flow and decision processes, the differences among employees and the reward system within the broad scope of work design of the individual.

Job analysis is the process of obtaining information about jobs. Job redesign makes use of job analysis to redefine a job in terms of tasks, behaviours, education, skills, relationships and responsibilities required.

C. Survey Feedback: A major difficulty in relying solely on sensitivity training is that it neglects the important procedural aspects of the functioning of teams. While the team members may get along with each other better as a result of the sensitivity training, in most cases, they will not become more effective unless there is an improvement in their actual procedures and the way they go about solving their problems.

To redress the balance, another approach to team development has emerged, i.e. survey feedback. This approach, first developed at the Institute of Social Research, University of Michigan, aims to get teams in organization to devise better processes for handling the issues facing them. Although consultants differ in how they apply survey feedback approach, they usually require the team to spend some time in a highly concentrated activity. Usually from two to three days, away from the working situation, it helps in examining how it goes about its tasks of setting objectives, making decisions, tackling problems etc.

The survey feedback approach is most effective at improving teams whose members already possess a high degree of conceptual skill and are dealing with long-term issues.

D. Process Consultation: Process consultation includes "a set of activities on the part of a consultant which help the client to perceive, understand and act upon process and events which occur in the client's environment". Process consultation assumes that an organization's effectiveness depends on how well its people relate to one another. An organization's problems, therefore, often can be traced to the breakdown of critical human processes at key places. Process consultation concentrates on certain specific areas such as communication, functional roles of members, group problem solving and decision-making, group norms and growth, leadership and authority, and inter-group cooperation and competition.

The assumptions underlying the process consultation model are:

1. Managers often need special diagnostic help in knowing what is wrong with the organization.
2. Most managers have constant desire to increase organizational effectiveness, but they need help in deciding 'how' to achieve it.
3. Managers can be effective if they learn to diagnose their own strengths and weaknesses without exhaustive and time consuming study of the organization.
4. The outside consultant cannot learn enough about the culture of the organization to suggest reliable new courses for action. He should, therefore, work jointly with the members of the organization.

E. Team Building: Team building is an attempt to assist the work group in learning how to identify, diagnose and solve its own problems. It directly focuses on the identification of problems relating to task performance and lays down concrete plans for their elimination. A team building programme deals with new problems on an ongoing basis. It is an effective technique by which members of an organizational group diagnose how they work together and plan changes that will improve their effectiveness.

9.2 Organizational Change

Change is the law of nature. Man has to encounter changes throughout his life. He has to mould himself continuously to meet new demands and face new situations. Despite the fact that change is a persistent phenomenon, it is a common experience that man resists change whether in the context of his pattern of life or in the context of his situation in an organisation. Here, we are concerned with the changes in business organisation. Management is the controller administration of the business organisation hence it has to face resistance to change from employees who are human beings. Hence, the problem of change management becomes significant.

9.2.1 Meaning of Organisational Change: The term 'organisational change' implies the creation of imbalances in the existing pattern of situation. When a business organisation operates and functions for a long time, an adjustment between its technical, human and structural set up is established. Organisation tends to approximate an equilibrium in relation to its environment. In other words, people (member) evolve a tentative set of relations with their environment. They have an adjustment with their job, working conditions, friends and colleagues etc. i.e. change requires individuals to make new adjustments. Hence, the fear of adjustment gives rise to the problem of change and resistance to change. Individual members can resist either individually or in groups. Individual resistance occurs when the job, remuneration, satisfaction or promotion etc., of an individual comes in danger. On the other hand, groups resist the change when their existence is in danger or a total change in overall work environment is contemplated.

9.2.2 Types of Changes in an Organisation: The change in an organisation may be of various types, like:

A. Changes Relating to Work: Such changes include the changes in machinery, working hours, method of work, job enlargement or sub-dividing or consolidating the jobs, etc. As is evident, these are mainly technical changes.

B. Change Relating to Organisation: Such changes are of social nature. They may relate either to a change in employee due to transfers, promotion, retrenchment or layoff, sub-division of jobs and restructuring in the organisation, change in informal groups, etc. Such changes require new social and environmental adjustments on the part of employees.

Joseph Massie has discussed the following types of changes in the management field.

1. **Changes in Knowledge, Information and Techniques:** The profession of management has its deep roots in the engineering problems of production. The technical aspect of the management field is advancing greatly. New techniques of production are being invented. Now a great deal of research is being conducted in various institutions of the world on behavioural science. It is recognised that wherever a manager must deal with other persons, some aspect of behavioural science comes into play. Therefore, the application of behavioural science to the management field is getting a top priority.
2. **Changes in the Scope of Management:** The writings of early management thinkers were primarily concerned with technical problems and their solutions. But with the passage of time, it was thought that process of management has universal application. Many problems in different types of organisations like industrial, educational, religious, hospital, etc., are common and they call for the application of certain management principles. This has broadened the scope of management and given birth to the

demand for specialisation of the application of management knowledge.

3. **Changes in the Issues and Problems Facing Managers:** There has been a great change both in magnitude and number in the problems before present day managers. These changes are caused by the emergence of large scale organisations and the separation of management from ownership. Moreover, there has been an awakening of the working class. Trade unionism has spread throughout the world. Consumers have also become conscious about their power over the organisation.
4. **Changes in Environment:** The world is changing fast. Population changes are becoming extremely significant to managers. Other changes can be viewed as changes in consumers, factors of production, social conditions, political conditions and economic trends. The increase in the size of consumer markets and the segmentation of markets into strata has changed the business environment. Consumption patterns are changing widely and managers continually search for market information to help them make sound decisions. Values, expectations and aspirations are continually being transformed.

9.2.3 Reasons for Changes: Changes in organisations are a must whether done deliberately and successfully or unwillingly. Some changes are visible while some others are invisible. In an organisation, the reasons for change may be as under:

1. Changes in business conditions.
2. Changes in managerial personnel.
3. Deficiencies in existing organisational patterns.
4. To keep the organisation from developing inertia.
5. Psychological reasons.

Thus, we see that changes in organisations may occur due to many reasons. For example, if there is a decline in the demand for the products of a firm, it may cause the management to plan for newer products, introduction of new technology or purchase of a new machinery or equipment, etc. Any new idea if implemented, will bring changes in the working of organisations. Similarly, the establishment of personal loyalty is dangerous for the smooth working of an organisation and achievement of common objectives. Hence, a change in the relationships among people becomes necessary. It is one of the important reasons for resistance why people in organisations experience difficulties in adjusting themselves to change in technology and work-relationship due to a break in their social interaction. Changes require individuals to make new adjustments. Hence, the great fear of non-adjustments or need of additional efforts required for adjustment creates resistance to change. Man is always feared of unknown and a change always has an element of uncertainty.

9.2.4 Change Resisted in an Organisation: Change is a continuous and natural process. It is a necessary thing for the survival and growth of business enterprises. For an enterprise's success, it may be necessary to forecast change in order to take advantages of the opportunities offered. However, since people resist to change, it must be an objective for the management to study the sources and causes of resistance to change, to overcome the resistance, to build in the organisation an awareness of change and to develop an ability in itself to forecast it and also to form an attitude of welcome change.

The basic problem in the management of change is the study of causes of resistance to change. Despite the fact that change is a persistent phenomenon, it is a common experience that men resist change whether in the context of their pattern of life or in the context of their situations in the organisation. Change of any type requires a readjustment while it is not simple, possible and favourable to all. Hence, resistance to change is also very usual as the change itself. To quote, "man has always feared the unknown and a change represents the unknown".

Some of the important reasons why people resist change in organisations are as follows:

A. Economic Reasons:

1. **Fear of Reduction in Employment:** Due to the change in technology, methods or work, quantity or quality of work, people think that there will be a cut in their emolument as they will not be able to cope with the change. This fear leads to the resistance for change on the part of people.
2. **Fear of Unemployment:** Generally, change in technology is expected to result in technical unemployment as old employees may not be able to handle new machines. Hence, the fear of unemployment leads to resistance to change. Such resistance is made both individually as well as in groups also. Opposition of automation is an example of it.
3. **Fear of Demotion:** Employees may fear that they may be demoted if they do not possess the new skills required for their jobs after the introduction of change. Hence, they prefer status quo.
4. **Fear of Increased Work Load:** Change in work technology and methods may lead to the fear that work load will be increased while there will be no corresponding increase in their wages. This feeling creates resistance to change.

B. Personal Reasons:

1. **Need of Training etc.:** If changes in technology and work organisation necessitate training and relearning on the part of employees, it may lead to resistance as all do not like to go for refresher and training courses off and on.
2. **Boredom and Monotony:** If the proposed change is expected to lead to greater specialisation resulting in boredom and monotony, it may also be resisted by people.
3. **No Participation in Change:** Some employees resist any change as they are critic of the situation that they have not been given any part in decision-making process for change. When they do not understand fully the implications of change they resist it. Some employees resist change on the ground as it implies a criticism of present method as inadequate or unsuitable.

C. Social Reasons:

1. **Need for New Social Adjustment:** Any organisational change requires new social adjustment with the group, work situation and new boss etc. All individuals are not ready to accept this challenge. Some people even refuse promotion due to this reason only as they will have to break their present socialites.
2. **Taking Change as Imposed from Outside:** Some employees take any change as imposed from outside upon them. This happens particularly when change is brought about abruptly. If employees are consulted and given due participation in the process of introducing change, then their objection and resistance can be minimised.
3. **Other Considerations:** Some employees may consider every change for the benefit of the management and company itself rather than their fellow workers or even the general public. Hence, they resist the change.

10

Participation and Empowerment

10.1 Meaning of Participation

The word participation is analysis differently by different groups such as labour, management, and the general public. For management, it is joint consultation prior to decision-making, for workers it means co-determination, while for government it is an association of labour with management without the final authority or responsibility in decision-making. Participation is conceived of as a way of reducing power difference between the management and workers in an organization. The degree of participation in an organization may be determined from the following indicators:

1. The amount of interaction between a supervisor and his subordinates.
2. The degree to which a supervisor performs his role in a group-centred way.
3. The degree to which a supervisor is active in making decisions and setting goals for his work units.

10.2 Levels of Participation

V.G. Mhetras has suggested five levels of participation in decision-making which range on a scale from minimum to maximum degree of participation. These are briefly discussed below.

- **Informative Participation:** It refers to information-sharing, concerning balance sheet, economic condition of the plant etc. Here, the workers have no right for close scrutiny of the information provided.
- **Consultative Participation:** The joint council is consulted on such matters as welfare programmes, and methods of work and safety. However, the final decision is always that

of the management, the council only works as an advisory body.

- **Associative Participation:** The role of joint council is not purely advisory unlike consultative participation. The management is under a moral obligation to accept and implement the unanimous decisions of the joint council.
- **Administrative Participation:** Under this, a decision already taken comes to the council with alternatives for it to select from for implementation of the decision. The degree of sharing authority and responsibility is definitely more than in the others.
- **Decision Participation:** Under this type of participation, decisions are taken jointly on matters relating to production, welfare, etc.

10.3 Process of Participation

Many of the modern organizations have programs of participation and empowerment of employees to gain several outcomes or advantages such as greater productivity, better quality, low costs, creative employees and satisfied workforce. The participative programs include joint consultation, suggestion schemes, co-partnership, quality circle etc. The programs of participation result in mental and emotional involvement that produces generally favourable outcomes for both the employees and the organization. Generally, participating employees are more satisfied with work than their supervisors, and their self-efficacy rises due to their new found empowerment.

The degree of participation in an organization may be determined by the following factors:

- The amount of interaction between a supervisor and his subordinates.
- The degree to which a supervisor performs his role in a group-centred way.
- The degree to which a supervisor is active in making decisions and setting goals for his work unit.

10.4 Mental and Emotional Involvement

Effective participation implies mental and emotional involvement. A person's entire self is involved, not just one's skill. This involvement is psychological rather than physical. A person who participates is ego-involved instead of merely task-involved. Some managers mistake task involvement for true participation. A manager may hold meetings, ask opinions, and so on, but all the time it is perfectly clear to employees that their manager is an autocratic boss who wants no ideas. This is pseudo-participation, not real participation. Employees fail to become ego-involved.

Participative programs motivate people to contribute. They are empowered to release their own resources of initiative and creativity towards the objectives of the organization, just as theory Y predicts. In this way, participation differs from "consent". The practice of consent uses only the creativity of the manager who brings ideas to the group for the members' consent. The consenters do not contribute; they merely approve. Participation is more than getting consent for something that has already been decided. Its great value lies in the fact that it tops the creativity of all employees. Participation especially improves motivation by helping employees understand and clarify their path towards goals. According to the path-goal model of leadership, the improved understanding of path-goal relationship produces a higher responsibility for goal attainment.

10.5 Methods of Workers' Participation

Several methods have been suggested and tried for ensuring worker's participation in management. The most important among them are mentioned below:

- **Co-Partnership:** Co-partnership makes the workers, shareholders in the company for which they are working. In this way, the workers become part-owners of the concern and acquire hand in its internal management. They may be able to elect their representative to the board of directors and thus participate in the management of the concern.

- **Suggestions Scheme:** To maintain employees' interest in the problems at the work place, suggestions scheme can be used with advantage. The management may invite suggestions from the workers for improvement in the existing set up and agree to pay suitable sums of money by way of rewards to the workers whose suggestions prove really useful. The payment may bear some proportion to the value of the suggestion in terms of improvement brought about or profit reaped. Such schemes are useful because they provide not only some new ideas to the management but also a feeling of importance to the workers.
- **Joint Consultation:** Joint consultation involves the setting up of joint committees comprising the representatives of management and workers to discuss various matters concerning working conditions of the workers. The decisions of such joint committees are usually advisory in nature. Generally, questions relating to wages, bonus, and piece rates are excluded from the scope of the committees. These matters are considered to be the subject matter of collective bargaining.
- **Management by Objectives:** Under managing by objectives, the subordinates are given freedom to set goals/targets for themselves for a given period. Each subordinate discusses his goals with the superior and both lay down benchmarks for measurement of results. It is an integral part of the participative management style under 'Theory Y' suggested by Douglas M.C. Gregor.

11

Financial and Non-financial Incentives

Management is the art of getting the work done through and with the people in formally organized groups. So, the main task of management is to motivate the employees to contribute their maximum towards the accomplishment of work. Generally, it is seen that workers produce only 60-70 percent of their capacity and if they are given some additional attraction or in other words 'incentive' of any kind, they work more. This increase in their work is due to the incentive given by the management to the workers. As a matter of fact, work result and incentives, have direct or positive correlation with each other.

11.1 Incentives Defined

Dr. Earnest Dichter has defined 'incentive' as follows: "Incentive is a stimulus of a reason for producing action. Almost all of the human motivations can serve as incentives—anxiety, worries, fear, hope, prestige, money, security and so on are all actual of potential incentives in our daily life". Thus, incentive is a stimulus for more work. It incites action, motivate the people to do more and more work to increase their efficiency and to learn newer techniques of work.

Incentive may be defined as any reward of benefit given to the employee over and above his wage or salary with a view to motivating him to excel in his work. Incentives include both monetary as well as non-monetary rewards. A scheme of incentive is a plan to motivate individual or group performance.

The following are some of the definitions of the term incentive:

- Wage incentives are extra financial motivation. They are designed to stimulate human effort by rewarding the person, over and above the time rated remuneration, for improvements in the present or targeted results.

- It refers to all the plans that provide extra pay for extra performance in addition to regular wages for a job -Hummel and Nickerson.
- It is any formal and announced programme under which the income of an individual, a small group, a plant workforce or all the employees of a firm are partially or wholly related to some measure of productivity output -Scott.

11.2 Need for Incentives

It is true that monetary compensation does constitute very important reason for the working of an employee. But this compensation alone cannot bring job satisfaction to the workers. One cannot expect effective performance from a worker who is dissatisfied with its job, even if he is well paid. Sociologists and industrial psychologists also view that the financial aspect is not the only dominant motivating force. Confidence in the management, pride in the job and in firm and concern for the overall good cannot be brought by a bonus. Hence, the modern authorities on management science have recognized the need for the provision of incentives to build up good morale.

Incentives can take any form. According to Z. Clark Dickinson, the important incentives for work can be listed as follows:

- Desire for livelihood and fear of want.
- Desire for approval of master and fear of punishment.
- Desire for praise and fear of being dismissed.
- Impulse to activity or joy in work and dislike of inactivity.
- The moral command and fear of conscience.

11.3 Merits of Incentives

The following are the advantages derived by providing incentives to employees:

- **Higher Output:** By providing incentives to his employees, the employer is able to induce them to work better. This leads to higher output.

- **Greater Profits:** Needless to say, higher output results in greater profits for the business. This happens in two ways. First, the cost per unit becomes less and second, the enterprise is able to keep the selling price low and it results in greater sales.
- **No Problem of Idle Time:** In an organisation where no proper incentives are available for the workers, the tendency will be to while away the time. When suitable incentives are available, the workers become time conscious. They begin to see every minute in terms of money.
- **Supervision Does Not Pose Any Problem:** When suitable incentives are available, the workers become duty conscious. The need for close supervision, thus, does not arise.
- **Efficient Workers are Able to Earn More:** Such of those workers who are highly efficient are able to earn more by way of performance bonus, higher commission and so on.
- **Possible to Identify Inefficient and Dull Workers:** If, in spite of the incentive schemes, some workers are able to earn only their normal wage, it should mean that they are basically dull. The employer, therefore, has to decide whether to retain them or subject them to rigorous training.
- **Rate of Labour Turnover is Bound to be Low:** If adequate incentives are available to the workers, they may not have a feeling of dissatisfaction. Such workers are sure to have greater work commitment and therefore may not leave the organisation. The rate of labour turnover, as a result, is bound to be low.
- **Reduction in Complaints and Grievances:** As the organization makes available suitable incentives to the workers, they may not have anything to complain about. This leads to reduction in complaints and grievances.

11.4 Problems Arising Out of Incentives

The following problems are bound to arise while

implementing an incentive plan:

- **Quality of Work May Suffer:** The workers, those in the production department in particular, may give undue importance to the quantity of output produced neglecting the quality of output. Such a problem can be overcome only if the organization has a perfect system of quality control.
- **Inter-personnel Relationships May Suffer:** Only those employees who are really efficient will be benefited out of incentives. This may promote ill-feelings among the employees of an organization.
- **Wear and Tear of Machines May be More:** As the employees are keen on increasing the output all the time, they may handle the machines carelessly. This increases the wear and tear of machines.
- **Health of the Workers May Get Affected:** Some workers tend to overwork in order to earn more and this may affect their health.
- **Increase in Accidents:** There is always a preference to step up output disregarding even safety regulations and this may increase the rate of accidents in the workplace.
- **Increase in Paper Work:** Proper administration of any incentive scheme involves lot of paper work. It necessitates the maintenance of proper records and books.

11.5 Requirements of a Sound Incentive Plan

A good incentive plan shall fulfil the following requirements:

- **Trust and Confidence:** The success of any incentive plan depends on the existence of an atmosphere of trust and confidence between the workers and the management. In the absence of such an atmosphere, the workers may resist any such proposal by the management.
- **Consensus Required:** The management should not take a unilateral decision while evolving an incentive scheme. Consensus between the workers and the management is

necessary for the success of the plan.

- **Assured Minimum Wage:** Payment to any worker should not be totally related to his performance. Every worker should be assured of a minimum wave notwithstanding performance. Only then the workers would have a sense of security.
- **No scope for Bias or Favouritism:** The standards set under the incentive plan should be based on objective analysis. It should not expect too much out of the employee nor should it give scope for bias or favouritism.
- **Simple to Operate:** The incentive plan should not involve tedious calculations. It should be so simple that the worker will be in a position to work out his total earnings himself.
- **Beneficial to Both the Workers and the Management:** The incentive plan should be beneficial to both the workers and the management. From the management's point of view, it should be cost effective. From the worker's point of view, it should offer return, at a rate higher than the normal rate of wages, for the extra efforts made by them.
- **Sound System of Evaluation:** A perfect system of evaluating the employees' performance should be created in the organisation. The results of evaluation should be made known to the employees at the earliest.
- **Redressing Grievances:** Grievances and complaints are bound to arise whenever any incentive plan is in vogue in the organisation. Proper machinery should be installed for the quick handling of all such complaints.
- **Review:** The progress of the incentive scheme should be periodically reviewed. Only then it would be possible to notice and remove defects, if any, in the plan.

11.6 Classification of Incentives

Incentives can be classified as follows:

11.6.1 Positive and Negative Incentives: Positive incentives are those incentives which induce a worker to work more. They exercise good effect on the morale and efficiency of the worker. Appreciation, recognition and promotions are the frequent examples of such incentives. On the other hand, negative incentives incite production by creating feeling of fines, fear and punishment. They motivate an individual to abstain from doing something, such as avoiding breakages, absenteeism and so on.

11.6.2 Financial and Non-financial Incentives: Money in itself has to value for man but in the context of the existing economic organisation, money has become a means not only satisfying the physical needs of daily life but also of obtaining social position, status and power. For this reason, financial incentives have assumed great importance. Financial incentives are offered in industries in two ways either in the form of salary increase or in the form of occasional bonus. They may be individual as well as group incentives, positive as well as negative too.

On the other hand, non-financial incentives are non-monetary social or psychological incentives. They all satisfy the inner-man of an employee and incite him to accomplish the best and more work. This is a well established fact now that a man does not work for the bread alone hence they are not satisfied with mere wages only. They require certain non-financial incentives also which satisfy their social, personal and psychological needs. Many people continue to do some work because it is more pleasant and enjoyable. This is a non-financial incentive. The non-financial incentive can also be personal or collective (group) incentives.

11.6.3 Individual and Group Incentives: When any incentive scheme is applied on personal basis or individual to individual, it is called individual incentive. This has the objective to give more profit to one who works more. On the other hand, group incentives are given to the group as a whole, to the people of a department or to all employees working within the organisation. Profit sharing, co-partnership and annual bonus schemes are the examples of group incentives.

11.7 Financial Incentives

Financial incentives or pecuniary incentives are the most original of all the incentives. It is given in the form of money. The financial incentives still form the most important influencing and motivating factor up to a certain limit. Because it is only by virtue of the monetary compensation that the workers can satisfy their fundamental needs such as food, clothing, shelter etc. The financial incentives may be either direct or indirect. Direct incentives include wages, bonus and other incentives directly given to the workers in the form of cash. Indirect financial incentives include subsistence allowance expenses, medical expenses etc.

This is an important, growing and alive controversy whether financial incentives are more important or non-financial incentives are more significant—accordingly, the workers should be given financial or non-financial incentives. Some authors as well as practicing managers give more importance to financial incentives. They claim that money in itself has no value for man but in the context of the existing economic organisation, money has become a means not only of satisfying the physical needs of daily life but also of obtaining position and power.

For this reason, financial incentives have assumed great importance. On getting money, man first turns his attention towards the things he needs—food, clothes, houses, etc. and then he satisfies the needs of health and education. Once these needs have been satisfied, he tries to obtain more and more luxuries. But some individuals continue to work even after having reached this stage because their social prestige and power increase with their bank balance. Individuals with this lust for money continue their search throughout their life—for this search never ends. People who do not feel any specific need for power do not like to earn money once their needs and comforts have been taken care of. In the same way, economic loss has diverse effects.

Loss of money deprives the poor man of his bread while the rich man loses his prestige although he does not suffer from hunger. Despite this, the poor man suffers less on account of this loss psychologically because only his body is directly affected. On the other hand, the rich man suffers a blow to his social prestige and self-respect, which is a mental injury. Money has become the means of satisfying many needs because it is the medium of exchange. If social position and power are not based on money in any society, then money will cease to be a powerful incentive. In communist countries, for example, since the abolition of private property, social respect has been the result, meaning that although there is no possibility of exchanging one's private property, individuals continue to work hard.

Money is the most important incentive in a society where a man's success is measured by the money he earns. But where this does not happen, money is not a powerful incentive. This analysis shows the importance of financial incentives. Financial incentives are offered in industries in two ways—either in the form of salary increase or in the form of occasional bonus. The financial incentives have the effect of increasing production and inducing the worker to work harder and better.

11.8 Non-financial Incentives

Non-financial or non-pecuniary incentives include all other influences planned or unplanned, which stimulate exertion. Mere monetary incentive cannot help the management in solving all the problems of industrial unrest. Further, additional cash wage may also tempt the workers to misuse the money in vices like gambling, drinking etc. Under such circumstances, the non-financial incentives have a significant role to play. Such incentives create a healthy atmosphere and change the mental outlook of the workers. They make the working class more stabilized and economically sound. Thus, in short, the workers by virtue of the non-financial incentives are enabled to enjoy a richer and fuller life. Experiences of foreign countries, particularly countries like Britain, America and Japan, have shown that there is a high degree of positive correlation between non-financial benefit schemes and labour productivity.

11.8.1 Forms of Non-financial Incentives: Non-financial incentives can take a variety of forms. Some of the popular ones are given below.

A. Job Security: The management must try its best to create a sense of job security. There should be no risk of retrenchment, demotion and termination. Experiences have also shown that the productivity is less in those concerns where workers have no feeling of safety and security. But it is high in those concerns where they have a feeling of job security.

B. Recognition: Recognition of work is the essence of securing good work. Efficient people would naturally like to get recognition for their skill and excellence in their work. Such recognition can do many things that what a cash reward can do. Of course, it is not practicable for the superiors to praise everybody for every thing done by them. But the technique of praise must be practiced as far as possible.

C. Participation: Workers feel more satisfied when they are given an opportunity to raise their voice in handling the affairs of the enterprise. Since they actually take part in the decision-making, their cooperation is assured.

D. Sincere Interest in Subordinates as Individual Persons: The workers must be made to feel pride in their job. Various techniques can be employed to develop pride to work. Food products, dynamic leadership, fair treatment, ethical conduct etc. can effectively stimulate the worker's pride in their job and in the firm.

E. Pride in Job: The workers must be made to feel pride in their job. Various techniques can be employed to develop pride to work. Food products, dynamic leadership, fair treatment, ethical conduct etc. can effectively stimulate the workers pride in their job and in the firm.

F. Delegation of Responsibility: Delegation of rights and responsibilities to execute a given task often proves to be a strong motivating factor. By delegation, the superior trusts his workers and stimulates them to show better results.

G. Other Incentives: Other incentives like quick promotion, provisions of facilities for development and training, provision of labour welfare amenities etc. also have a significant role to play in motivating the employees.

11.8.2 Individual Non-financial Incentives: These are incentives which motivate people on individual basis. The various forms of individual motive are as follows:

A. Status: Status, in general terms, is the ranking of people in the society. In the organisational context, it means the ranking of position, right and duties in the formal organizational structure. Good status motivates the people to put more work and do better.

B. Promotion: Promotion is defined as a movement to a position in which responsibilities and presumably prestige are increased. Promotion satisfies the needs of human being in the organisation from various angles such as money, prestige, status and so on. The avenues of promotion, if they exist in the organisation, play an important role in motivating the employees.

C. Responsibility and Challenge: Many people prefer challenge and responsible job rather than monotonous and insipid jobs. The management should provide such opportunities also by making the work challenging and more responsible.

D. Making Job Pleasant and Interesting: The work should be made enjoyable and pleasant if it is so designed. It will allow the employees to satisfy their natural instincts. This creates interest in the work and employees make it a peculiar method of making work more interesting.

E. Recognition of Work: Most people have a need for a

high evaluation of themselves. They want that their work should be recognized by others. Recognition means acknowledgment with a work of appreciation. When such appreciation is given to the work performed by employees, they feel motivated to perform work at similar or higher level.

11.8.3 Collective Non-financial Incentives: Employees work in groups. Their efficiency, aspiration, behavioural norms and standards are affected by the group. If the group in general is efficient, an employee tends to become more efficient. Hence, group incentives are also important. Some of the collective non-financial incentives are as follows:

A. Social Importance of Work: People generally prefer a job which is socially acceptable. If the society gives importance and praise to the work, people like to perform. Sometimes, people prefer a job of high social importance even though the financial compensation would be less. The reason is simple. People have to live in the society and by performing a job of high social importance, the drive satisfaction of being important in the society is enhanced.

B. Team Spirit: The management should encourage team spirit, that is, to work in cooperation and coordination. Team work is a coordinated action by a cooperative small group in regular contact wherein members contribute responsibly and enthusiastically towards the task achievement. If there is team spirit among the employees, they will try to put in maximum efforts to achieve the objective.

C. Competition: Sometimes, for providing incentives to employees, competitions are organised between different individuals or different groups. There may be a case of self-competition where an individual tries to improve his earlier performance. When an individual performs very well because of such competition, he should be given some advantages, not necessarily in terms of money, but may be in terms of recognition, prestige, praise, etc. However, this method has a negative consequence also. Though all the employees try to put in maximum efforts, all of them cannot win. As such they may feel frustrated and their efficiency can go down. Hence, there is a need to have only healthy competition.

D. Informal Groups: When people work together, they develop some sort of affiliation among themselves. These relationships are not officially prescribed, but created on the basis of certain factors, both personality factors of the employees and other social factors. Creation of these informal groups provides social satisfaction to employees at work place. People feel to achieve a sense of belongingness and security. Management should provide the way of creation of such informal groups so long as they are not detrimental to organisational efficiency and objectives because sometimes, the informal groups may go against the interest of the organisation.

11.8.4 Institutional Non-financial Incentives: The incentives are related with the environmental factors in the organisation. Conductive and congenial atmosphere of the organisation motivates employees to produce better results. Following incentives fall in this category.

A. Human Relation in Industry: Human relation in the industry is related with the policy to be adopted in the organisation to develop a sense of belongingness in the employees, improve their efficiency and treat them as human beings and not merely a factor of production. The emphasis is on providing greater satisfaction, both physiological and psychological, by creating such environment in the organisation where employees are able to work efficiently. In such an environment, employees are motivated to stay with the organisation and they also inculcate a productive behaviour.

B. Participation: The superior-subordinate relationship emphasises that superior takes the decisions and subordinate implements them. However, in such a decision-making process, subordinate does not feel very enthusiastic in implementing the decisions. As such, the subordinate should also be associated with the decision-making process. This not only motivates a subordinate to take prompt and proper action on decision implementation, but also makes him responsible for anything which goes wrong.

C. Communication: Communication is the lifeline of an organisation. Complex nature and big size of organisations require greater specialisation and division of work. Thus, for a particular goal, total activities are divided into parts and sub-parts to share the information about their functioning among themselves. This is done through communication as communication is the process of passing ideas and understanding from one person of group to other person or group. A free and adequate flow of communication is necessary. This, besides providing base for successful organisational functioning, also provides satisfaction to individuals in the organisation as they want to be informed properly about the matters concerning their interests. Thus, proper communication in the organisation motivates employees properly.

D. Discipline: Discipline is in essence obedience, application, energy behaviour and outward makes of respect shown by employees. It is employees' self-control to meet organisation's standards one objectives. Management has primary responsibility for developing and maintaining discipline. It maintains discipline by applying standards in a consistent, fair and flexible manner. This provides employees to behave in a particular direction as any employee whose behaviour is inconsistent with standards, invites disciplinary action.

11.9 Group Incentives

Incentives can be of various types viz. positive and negative, individual and group incentives, monetary and non-monetary incentives and so on. When incentives are classified on the basis of number of the employees to whom the schemes are being applied, it can be personnel or individual and group or collective incentives. Individual incentives are provided to individuals in different ways while group incentives are applied to a group of employees collectively. From monetary point of view, group incentives can be of two types viz., financial as well as non-financial. Inviting suggestions from workers, workers' participation in management are two peculiar examples of non-financial group incentives. Profit-sharing, distribution of annual bonus, and distributing department prizes are some examples of group incentives.

11.9.1 Advantages of Group Incentives: Group incentives give the following benefits as compared to individual incentives:

- They develop a group feeling and sense of cooperation while struggles and difference of opinions die out.
- Group has no quick demand of job changes and everybody is engaged in the completion of the collective object.
- Group incentives put off the problems of absence and coming late.
- Because of group incentives, other managerial problems like transfer, decrease in labour promotion becomes less.
- The labour costs and production overheads are reduced.

11.10 Worker's Participation in Management

Worker's participation in management is an important form of non-financial incentive to the workers. It is an important change in the attitude of management as well as in human relation area. Association of labour with management in the management of the enterprise has become a necessity of the time. The increasing association of the workers with management offers an enormous potential for higher productivity, improved job satisfaction, satisfying the worker's urge for self-expression, industrial peace, better industrial relations and so on.

11.10.1 Worker's Participation Defined: The term worker's participation is variously understood by different parties. Management interprets it as the joint consultation prior to decision-making; workers regard it as co-decision and right of co-determination; academicians view it practically as association of labour without the final authority or responsibility in decision-making. It is also considered as a system of communication and consultation by which employees of an organisation are kept informed about the affairs of the company and through which they express their opinion as regards the problems of industry and contribute to management decisions.

Thus, it aims at sharing in an appropriate manner, the decision-making power with the workers in an organisation. This sharing of decision-making power or participation in management, makes workers mentally and emotionally involved in a group situation which encourages them to contribute to the group goals and share responsibility with them.

Thus, the essence of the plan of worker's participation in management is essentially a recognition of the human aspect of the organisation and gives them (i.e., the workers) an equal opportunity and platform to discuss and decide over the problems of the industry.

11.10.2 Forms of Worker's Participation: Worker's participation in management may take various forms but the following three forms are more appropriate and common in this connection.

A. Co-partnership: In this form of participation, the workers become the co-partners or shareholders in the company. Being member of the company, they take active part in policy framing like other shareholders and decide over the matters. These shares can be allotted to them by the way of bonus or through direct subscription. Sometimes, the workers may be allowed to purchase shares in an enterprise at concessional rate. However, subscription to share capital makes it feasible for the workers to become part owners of the concern and share in the decision-making power of the concern.

B. Appointment of Labour Directors: In this system, board of directors have one or two representatives as directors who enjoy the same status, rights and powers as other elected directors. They may be nominated either by trade unions or elected through any other system by workers. Sometimes, they may be nominated by the management also. However, the system is not very effective because labour directors being in minority, cannot influence the decisions of the board of directors. They can put only their opinions and insist on a particular view point. This system was initially started in England and then exercised in other European countries but no hopeful success had been achieved in this direction. In India also, the system has been tried in some establishments but with no positive success.

C. Joint Consultative Committees or Work Committees: In this method, a joint committee or worker's representatives as well as of management is constituted in the organisation. These committees may be set up at various levels, such as plant level and industry level, etc. These committees consider and discuss problems of labour, working conditions and terms of work, etc. Separate committees are formed for problems. These committees generally work in advisory capacity only but because they consist of the representatives of both the groups, the management nearly accepts the recommendations of both parties and agree to these decisions being a party to it.

Such joint consultations are a step towards increasing productivity of workers, sound industrial relations and improving the morale amongst the workers. In India, number of JCMSs has been established in various industrial enterprises but their progress has been very moderate.

11.10.3 Objectives of Participation: Generally, a number of arguments are put forth by the workers (or their representatives) to advocate the case for their participation in the management. They can be summarized under the following three main themes—economic, social and psychological. The objectives are actually a corollary of the different basis of participation and quite common too. Hence, we can discuss the objects of worker's participation in management under these three sub-heads.

The economic objectives as served by participation deals

with the productivity aspect directly, which aims at enhancing the progress and prosperity of the industrial concern. The increased productivity is possible only when there exists a fullest cooperation between labour and capital. It has empirically been tested that poor labour management relations do not encourage the workers to contribute anything more than the minimum desirable to retain their jobs.

The social objectives of participation are reflected in terms of maintaining healthy industrial relations by reducing industrial strifes and creating positive conditions in which industrial harmony and peace can grow. Industrial peace is maintained by this instrument when it helps substituting homogeneity of objects and is common place in lieu of diverse and conflicting interests between the parties. In participation, a spirit of trust and cooperation rather than suspicion and rivalry governs the relationship of management and labour to one another. Similarly, it creates pleasant atmosphere for maintaining industrial peace.

Psychological objectives are concerned to secure full recognition of the human element in industry. Association of workers with management provides them with a sense of importance and involvement and self-expression. He considers himself to be an indispensable constituent of the organisation, which creates a feeling of belonging in his mind and, therefore, he invests his life in the organisation. All these factors contribute to a sound foundation for human relations in the industry.

11.10.4 Advantages of Worker's Participation: In modern times, it is very different to do anything without the responsive involvement of the workers. Hence, the idea of worker's participation in management has assumed greater importance. Nowadays, it has become an essential step to improve industrial relations. The importance, need or significance of this scheme can be illustrated from the following facts.

A. Increase in Mutual Understanding: In the modern industrial economies, management and labour are two opposite forces and they look at other with doubts and mistrust. They do not know about the problems of other side and nor do they try to know it. The scheme of worker's participation in management brings them closer and provides them a common platform to discuss the problems of the enterprise with each other. It increases mutual faith and good understanding among them.

B. Increase in Production: By participation of workers in management, there will be an increasing goodwill and cooperation which is a pre-condition for more production. Without industrial cooperation we cannot expect an increase in production and productivity.

C. Industrial Peace: This scheme ends the sense of mistrust in workers as the both parties understand each other's problems. Hence, no struggle occurs. It brings industrial peace and harmony in the industrial field.

D. Way of Self-expression: This scheme is an important form of self-expression for the workers. Hence, it is an important non-financial and psychological motivation to the workers. Their ego and their 'inner-man' is satisfied when they speak on the affairs related to their problems. They do work with more interest, enthusiasm and willingness. Hence, the productivity is increased which is reflected in higher production and lowering down of the cost of production.

12

Industrial Psychology

Industrial psychology, as the name indicates, is that branch of psychology which studies human behaviour under industrial circumstances. Psychology is a normative science of behaviour which can be observed in the social, economic, educational and other spheres. In the modern period, different branches of psychology have been developed during the study of human behaviour in various fields. Educational psychology has been developed to study human behaviour in the field of education while social psychology is concerned with the study of human behaviour in a social environment. This is an age of industrial progress, in which each progressive nation is expanding the scope of its industries but industries cannot be made to function without human beings, because individuals are required in the capacity of managers, administrators and workers.

And, wherever there are human beings their behaviour will be influenced by their relationship. If, in the industrial field, human relations deteriorate, then the result would be strikes and lockouts which have a widespread impact on the economy of the nation. Since the future of every nation depends upon its industrial development and progress, this particular field of human behaviour becomes extremely important. It is the aim of industrial psychology to study the principles governing behaviour in the industrial field and to undertake research.

Psychology is not merely a theoretical science for it not only enunciates general laws concerning human behaviour but also tries to improve human life by applying these principles. Like any other science, therefore, psychology also has two aspects—the theoretical and the practical. Industrial psychology is naturally a branch of practical psychology because it is fundamentally a study evolved for the improvement of human relations in the industrial sphere. The knowledge provided by it is used to solve the problems of people who work in industry, as well as to solve these non-human problems which emerge from time to time in industries. Now-a-days, psychologists are appointed to study the problems which arise in the field of industrial psychology.

A glance at the history of industrial psychology will show that universities have been responsible for the research concerned with it, but even more important research has been carried on in big industries under actual conditions. It is, therefore, more appropriate to consider industrial psychology as a branch of practical psychology. This aspect of the subject can be even better understood by studying the following definitions.

12.1 Definitions of Industrial Psychology

Some of the main definitions of industrial psychology are the following.

According to Blum, a famous psychologist, industrial psychology is simply the application or extension of psychological facts and principles to the problems concerning human relations in business and industry. Blum shows in this definition that psychological facts and principles are used in human relations in the field of business and industry and this constitutes industrial psychology. By using them, the industrial psychology tries to solve the problems that arise in the industrial sphere. As Blum says further, industrial psychology provides practical solutions to the problems that arise in the industrial society and its economic organisation.

Harrell has defined the subject in his book titled 'Industrial Psychology' in the following words, "industrial psychology is the study of people at work in industry and business". In his opinion, industrial psychologists make a study of the behaviour of people working under conditions of business and industry. Harrell has further clarified that the subject matter of industrial psychology is always the human being because it is the human being who is the object of a psychological study. Even in a business or industrial environment, this continues to be true. Just as social psychology studies the human being under social circumstances, industrial psychology studies the individual in a business environment.

As Harrell himself has put it, 'individual psychology is a complicated study of a number of things, but it is always primarily the study of people as individuals or in groups—in work situations'.

It hardly needs to be explained that the individual psychologists focus their attention upon human beings.

Thus, from the above definitions, it is clear that industrial psychology is the branch of psychology which studies human behaviour in industrial circumstances. It studies physical as well as mental aspects of the work, behaviour of the people at work and the relationship of work and job satisfaction.

12.2 Scope of Industrial Psychology

Pointing out the scope of industrial psychology, Harrell has laid stress on the following things:

- Industrial psychology is concerned with the physical aspect of the environment of work, for example, the effect of life and temperature on work and safely.
- It is primarily a study of behaviour and principles of human relationship.
- It is a study of the causes that lead to indifference and disinterest and the motives and attitudes that influence zeal and high morale.
- It is a study of the methods by which neurotic people can be bought back to a level of normal health.
- It is a study of the factors that create cooperation between labourers and the management, a study of the relation between the supervisor and his subordinates and of industrial conflicts.

Briefly, the scope of industrial psychology is the following.

12.2.1 Economic Social and Psychology Aspects of Industry: Industrial psychology is concerned with human behaviour in the entire industrial environment. Consequently, it studies the economic, social and psychological aspects of human behaviour. In the modern age, most economic factors have some psychological influence. The various factors in the communal life of workers living in an industrial environment also influence the psychology of the workers. Industrial psychology studies this also.

12.2.2 Study of the Physical Aspect of Work Environment: In an industry, the worker is greatly influenced by the conditions under which he works. If the conditions are to his linking, the worker feels satisfied and remains healthy while on the other hand, if the conditions are not good, the number of accidents goes up and workers become dissatisfied. Working conditions include a number of factors such as clean air and water, arrangement of necessary rest, less noise, clean atmosphere, sufficient light, good relations between the worker and the management etc.

In all these, guidance by the psychologist can prove to be of immense value. For example, it is better to consult a psychologist about the arrangement for lighting, about the quantity or intensity of the light and the angle front which it should come from. Even the colour of the walls, floors and ceiling of the factory greatly influences the workers. It has been mentioned in experiments that if the colour scheme of the environment is good, there are fewer accidents and the atmosphere remains good. And it is for the psychologist to suggest what should be the colour of the machines, roofs, floors and ceilings. It can thus be said that industrial psychology studies the physical working conditions.

12.2.3 Principles of Human Relationships: Irrespective of the automation introduced in any industry, human element cannot be eliminated. Even the biggest and the most efficient machine needs an engineer to run it, and because the engineer is a human being, the importance of the psychological element in the running of the factory cannot be denied. The efficiency of the man will depend very much upon the nature of his relations with the management. In the last century, most industrialists behaved like autocrats and considered the workers as nothing more than tools. But in that period the level of efficiency was never very high. It has been seen that an industrialist can achieve a higher rate of production if he behaved sympathetically with his employees. In the present age, the industrialist can no longer do as he wills, because of the existence of labour unions.

An industrialist who cannot maintain good and cordial relations with his workers does not succeed for long. Being the science of behaviour, industrial psychology tries to discover principles for improving human relationships in an industrial environment. At the root of most of the lockouts and strikes, which are common forms of expressing discontent seen frequently in most industries today, are only distorted and injured human relationships. Industrial psychology helps to solve these problems.

12.2.4 Study of Aptitudes and Motives: As in any other circumstance, human behaviour in an industrial environment is influenced and formed by attitudes and motives. Behaviours change with the change in stimuli. Hence, it is necessary to study the rules pertaining to correct attitudes and motives. Industrial psychology pursues this kind of study. One example of a study of this kind is the study conducted by Hawthorne Works Western Electric Company to study the effect of the attitudes of workers upon production. This study is known as the Hawthorne study.

12.2.5 Study of Principles of Mental Health: Today, intelligent people realise the importance of maintaining the proper health of workers. The worker's mental health is profoundly influenced by the conditions under which he works and by the attitude of other people towards him. Industrial psychology studies the factors influencing the mental health of industrial workers and tries to discover principles for maintaining their mental health. Industrial psychology also gives suggestions for improving the mental health of workers who are suffering from mental disease and are unbalanced.

12.3 Problems of Industrial Psychology

12.3.1 Selection of the Right Man for the Right Job: If success is to be achieved in any industry it is essential that the right man should be found and appointed to the right job. This involves first an accurate work study and also the selection of the most qualified individual from among the applicant to suit that particular job. This is basically a problem for the psychologist because the selection involves many kinds of psychological tests to discover the various abilities of the individuals. It also happens sometimes that an individual working on a particular post cannot work efficiency for personal reasons, even though he is otherwise perfectly qualified to hold that post. In such a situation, the industrial psychologist is faced with the problem of giving suggestions which will once again render the individual fit for work.

12.3.2 Training for Workers: Although different individuals have varying degrees of ability to perform different kinds of functions, training can be useful in improving these abilities to such an extent that the individual becomes capable of doing work which could not have done without training. The kind and length of training required to train a particular individual to bring him up to a certain level of efficiency can be determined by the psychologist. Hence, another problem for the industrial psychologist is the training of workers.

12.3.3 Morale in Industry: Despite the best possible working conditions in an industry, the highest efficiency cannot be achieved unless the workers also have a high morale. Morale can be seen on the other hand in the enthusiasm and zeal with which work is tackled and on the other hand in the mutual cooperation extended to others in group activities. How a proper morale can be maintained in industry and what steps are necessary to create it is a problem for psychology, and it is the industrial psychologist who solves it.

12.3.4 Human Relations in Industry: The problem of human relations in industry has assumed greater importance and complexity with the formation of trade unions which have channelled the power of the workers into single channel. Now no industry can run successfully and smoothly for any length of time in the absence of good relations between the management and the worker's union. If the relations deteriorate, the level of production falls, accidents increase, and lockouts and strikes are the result. The problem of human relation is primarily the concern of social psychology and the person best equipped to solve it is the industrial psychologist.

12.3.5 Fatigue and Boredom: In industry, as in any other sphere of human activity, individuals become tired and bored after a long spell of mechanical work. Their psychological fatigue increases with this. Fatigue is both physiological and psychological. Scientifically viewed, the work and the instruments used in an industry should be so designed and planned as to result in the least possible amount of fatigue and the highest possible quantity of work. Specialists of engineering psychology have designed various kinds of machines and tools with this objectivity in view. They have also given many suggestions about the improvement of methods of work. Industrial psychologists have also conducted many experiments on mental fatigue and boredom, and given many valuable suggestions on the basis of their results. It has been observed, for example, that if there is arrangement for music and light entertainment in certain kinds of mechanical work, the extent of fatigue and problem is greatly reduced.

12.3.6 Industrial Accidents: If we want a machine to function without any accident, two things are necessary. In the first place the machine itself should be in good working order and in the second place, the worker maintaining it should be using it correctly, and his mental condition must be normal. For the first factor, engineering psychologists have given useful suggestions for keeping the machines functioning properly and without accidents. Regarding the second factor, they have given some suggestions for the development of safety habits, proper maintenance and the maintenance of normal mental health. Hence, one important problem before industrial psychology is the prevention of accidents.

12.3.7 Responses towards Physical Environment: It has already been pointed out that the physical conditions existing in an industry such as the quantity, quality and direction of light, arrangement for fresh and clean air, proper ventilation, hygiene, level of noise, the amount of humidity in the air, etc. have an important influence upon the efficiency of the worker. In order to find out the kind of conditions that should exist in a particular industry, it is necessary to find out the workers response to their environment. Clearly, it is the industrial psychology which can find out and determine the quantity and the quality of these physical conditions which are desirable.

12.3.8 Problems of Production: Maximum production in any industry can only be achieved under certain circumstances. Even if the machines are the best, it is essential that the worker handling them must also be capable. How can this ability be tested? In every factory, many machines are installed? How can one find the particular person best suited to operate each particular machine? And out of the many people who apply for a job in a factory, how can one discover the few who may prove to be really capable? In order to achieve maximum production, it is necessary that machines should be so designed as to include the minimum fatigue and the lighting so arranged to give the least possible strain to the workers. Besides, most people soon become bored with their work. How can their enthusiasm be reawakened? How should the factory work be designed so as to reduce the number of accidents? Psychology is needed to solve all these problems which beset every industry.

12.3.9 Problems of Selling: The work of an industry does not end with the production of things, but carries on till the produced goods are sold. If one does not get success in selling the final produce, its quality and quantity matter less than nothing. And in order to sell things, it is necessary that people should be acquainted with the product, its qualities and should develop the need to buy them. Advertisement serves the purpose, and successful advertisement is based on appeal. Hence, the value of psychology in the field of advertisement can hardly be disputed.

12.3.10 Prevention and Solution of Industrial Conflicts: No industry is completely free from quarrels and conflicts of a minor or major kind. At times, these conflicts get out of hand and lead to strikes by the workers or lockouts by the management. These are extreme cases in which such conflicts lead to widespread arson, gheraoes, murder and wilful destruction of public and private property. Although some economic demands or political factors may be at the root of such industrial conflicts, the most important factor influencing the action of workers and the management alike is the psychological element. This is why sometimes even great issues are overlooked so that no conflict occurs while relatively insignificant incidents like the impolite words of a manager to a worker may lead to strike and violent conflicts. It is the psychological factor which results in strikes and conflicts becoming extremely violent.

If such conflicts are to be resolved, mere satisfaction of economic demands is not enough. It is necessary also to remove those factors which, from the psychological standpoint, are responsible for the occurrence of such conflicts. If these psychological factors are kept in view from the beginning, it is possible to reduce the number of conflicts. And it is the task of industrial psychologists to study these factors.

The importance and value of the industrial psychologist's advice in big industrial complexes is evident from the above exposition of his role in solving problems of industry. It is for this reason that in all developed countries industrial psychologists are invariably employed in all large-scale industries.

12.4 Objectives of Industrial Psychology

As a branch of applied psychology, industrial psychology has the following objectives:

- **Personal Selection:** Industrial psychology tries to find out how a suitable individual can be selected to perform a particular task. If these can be done, then the work gets the correct worker where the worker himself gets the work he can do best.

- **Care of Workers' Health:** If the worker does not have good mental and physical health, the work of the industrial unit cannot progress smoothly. His mental and physical health is profoundly influenced by the conditions under which he is required to work and by his relations with the management. The objectives of industrial psychology are to discover the ideal conditions in which the best mental and physical health of the worker can be maintained.
- **Protection of Workers' Economic Interest:** Mental health cannot be maintained unless a person's economic interest is secure. Besides, the worker cannot be encouraged to give his best if he is uncertain about his economic condition. Hence, industrial psychology evaluates the efficiency of the worker and determines an adequate salary or suggests scientific principles on the basis of which an adequate salary can be determined.
- **Search for Proper Methods of Work:** One important reason for accidents and mishaps in factories is the improper methods of work. Improper working also promotes fatigue and boredom. Hence, another objective of industrial psychology is to find out the proper methods of work so that accidents are prevented and fatigue and boredom reduced to the minimum.
- **Removing Maladjustment:** Another important factor which causes industrial conflicts is the lack of adjustment between the worker and his circumstances and the conditions in which he works. This maladjustment is primarily psychological in nature. It is the task of the industrial psychologist to locate the cause of maladjustment and to suggest means of rectifying it. This is another objective of industrial psychology.
- **Reform of Working Conditions:** It is the task of the industrial psychology to find out the ideal conditions in which the highest efficiency can be attained and the

worker's productivity is maintained at the peak of mental and physical health. The most important working conditions include arrangement for adequate and proper lighting, proper ventilation, absence of noise, provision for periodical rest, normal conveniences for the male and female employees, etc.

- **Reform in Machines:** The worker and the machine are equally responsible for the number of accidents and amount of fatigue induced in the worker. Prevention of accident and reduction in fatigue can be achieved by the proper designing of machines. Industrial psychologist gives useful suggestions for the improvement of machines and tools.
- **Reform in Human Relationships:** In order to maintain a proper atmosphere and a high degree of morale among the workers in an industry, it is necessary to have proper and cordial human relations between the workers and the management. One objective of the industrial psychologist is to suggest means of improving human relations.
- **Humanistic Approach in Industry:** Psychologist studies have established that human relations industry cannot be good unless a humanistic approach is adopted. Hence, the relations existing between the management and the various level of workers should be improved and the barriers between them removed. Industrial psychologists help in spreading the humanistic approach in industry.

12.5 Value of the Study of Industrial Psychology

Progress in the field of industry depends not only on advances in technology but also upon the cordiality and pleasantness of human relations. In the field of industry, these human relations are also the industrial relations, and are fundamentally psychological in nature. They depend upon the interest, motives, sentiments, and passions of individuals. If their nature is to understand and they are to be made more profitable, it is necessary to undertake a study of interests, motives, sentiments and passions, which is the task of psychology. For this reason, psychological study in the sphere of industry is of great value. The following facts can be pointed out regarding the contribution of industrial psychology to industry.

12.5.1 Solution to Labour Problems: Conflicts between management and workers is almost a normal feature of every industry and can be caused by almost any factor. Often they become so violent that they result in severe losses in terms of money and lives to both the management and the workers. At the root of all such conflicts are some psychological tensions. It is the task of psychology to study these conflicts, and for that reason, psychology can help in finding solution to these problems. Most of the means adopted today to improve the relations between the management and the worker have in fact evolved from psychological observation and testing under actual industrial conditions over a long period of time. They cannot be changed by the wish of any one individual.

The truth of the matter is that a conflict can be resolved only if the various factors inherent in it are separated and analysed. Even in the sphere of industrial conflicts, only the psychologist can do this. One major cause of conflict, for example, is the individual differences between individuals which are studied by psychology. Just as a doctor is consulted in the case of bodily disease, and the sociologist consulted about social problems, the industrial psychologist should be considered a specialist on psychological problems in industry and his help should be sought.

12.5.2 Prevention of Accidents: Psychology has provided valuable suggestions not only in the solution of conflicts but also in the prevention of accidents. Psychologists have discovered the kinds of machines that should be designed, the manner in which they should be operated and the plan according to which they should be arranged in a factory. The purpose of this study is to find means for preventing accidents. The psychologist finds out how much accident prone the workers are and suggests methods of getting rid of this propensity.

12.5.3 Study of Aptitudes: Irrespective of the quality and nature of the physical conditions prevailing in a factory, it depends upon the worker's aptitude towards the work—it will get done but if his aptitude is not suitable then even the best conditions cannot persuade the worker to work. The study and measurement of aptitude is the subject of psychology and it is the psychologist who can help the industrialist here.

12.5.4 Maintaining Morale: In order to maintain a certain level of production and to improve the quality of production, it is necessary in every industry and profession to maintain a high level of morale among the workers. Morale is influenced by a large number of psychological factors such as affection and freedom, the desire to make sacrifices, availability of proper, leadership, etc. By studying these, psychologists can give suggestions for maintaining the right morale.

12.5.5 Creating Proper Leadership: The study of leadership is the responsibility of social psychology. In the field of industry, the supervisor must not only be an official but also a capable leader because otherwise he cannot guide the worker properly and encourage him to work hard. Social psychology can help in the field of industry by pointing out the qualities that are necessary for leadership and by explaining how such qualities can be developed. It can also tell the industrialist about the person who has qualities or who is capable of developing them.

12.5.6 Measurement of Individual Differences: Success of a profession in an industry can be achieved only if the most capable workers are assigned jobs which they are best capable of performing. If this can be done, the workers perform to their functions with interest and can thus increase production and improve the quality. Individual differences call only be discovered by a wide variety of psychological tests. Hence, the assistance of a psychologist can prove to be of great value in his sphere.

12.5.7 Study of Efficiency: Overall, all the workers are not expected to have the same degree of efficiency because there are many different kinds of functions to be performed, for which varying levels of efficiency and calibre is needed. The psychologists can find out which person has the efficiency to perform a particular job. In addition to this, a psychologist can also give suggestions for improving efficiency by removing those obstacles which hinder efficiency.

12.5.8 Use of Psychological Tests: In the present times, psychological test are being extensively employed to select the most qualified individuals for particular jobs in an industry. The chief tests are those of intelligence, interest, aptitude and personality. Sometimes many of these tests are included in a single test battery. Some of these tests are used on individuals while others are used to study the group qualities of workers. All these tests have their own limitations but even then they are successfully used in the recruitment of employees in an industry.

12.5.9 Motion and Times Studies: Different people take varying amount of times to complete a specific job because they work at different speed. Today, times and motion studies are conducted to find out the efficiency of individuals and even of machines. These studies have also been used to find out means by which a specific work can be done better in a shorter time. Labour and time is saved by analysing motion studies so that essential movements can be isolated and concentrated upon. Time studies help in economizing upon the time spent in a particular operation. In modern factories, the machines, the specific places at which particular workers sit and the positions in which they sit, are so arranged as to save time and to improve efficiency. All this is done to eliminate all unnecessary movement and duplication of work.

12.5.10 Aid in Industrial Training: It is now accepted that the efficiency of a worker can be appreciably improved by the proper kind of training and that the expense involved in training is paid off double fold. Trained people can avoid accidents while the quality and quantity of their production is far higher than that of untrained people. Hence, different kinds of training programmes for different jobs are now called for. At the same time, training programmes for workers at all level are now organised regularly. The industrialist stands to gain by all such training imparted to his employees. Such training programmes can be devised only by the psychologist who can point out the basis of such training and the methods in it.

12.5.11 Suggestion Concerning Motives: An employee must be motivated if he is to progress in his job. This motivation can be supplied through increase in wages, promotion, praise or in many other ways. In the absence of motivation or on account of disappointment, the quality upon the quantity of the workers and output, both suffer. The special study of motivation is the task of psychology. Only a psychologist can point how a worker can be motivated to improve the quality and quantity of his produce, how the workers and the motives can be prevented from leading them to strike; how wages should paid so as to constitute a permanent motive. All these suggestions tremendously help in the working of an industry.

12.5.12 Studies of Fatigue and Monotony: The most important obstacle in the way of increasing production is fatigue and monotony. Psychologists have conducted extensive studies into the cause of both and into the ways and means of eliminating them. These suggestions can be of great help in removing fatigue and monotony from industrial work.

It is clear from the above explanation that psychology has great importance for industry and this importance is increasing day by day.

12.6 Physical Conditions of Work

12.6.1 Intensity, Location, Distribution and Colour of Light: The kinds and intensity of light differs with the age of the workers as well as with the occupation that they have adopted. As a normal rule, individuals over 30 require light of a greater intensity than their younger counterparts. If the objects handled are minute, then naturally, the light must be fairly bright, while in work where objects handled are of a large size, and the workers are fairly young, intense light is not necessary. Light provided should never be intense enough to cause glare, and never dim enough to cause strain in concentrating upon an object to be worked upon. Work that requires light of high intensity also requires the use of special protected glasses, as is the case with welding where the light of a very high intensity is produced by the welding flame. Protection from its harmful effects is achieved by the use of coloured glasses.

The source of light should be so located as to avoid falling directly upon the eyes; instead, it should fall on the instrument that is to be designed and then also in a manner to avoid all reflection into the eyes of the person handling it. Hence, light should be evenly distributed and for this, tube lighting has been found to be superior to bulb lamps, which are now considered obsolete.

Daylight is naturally uniform in its distribution; it is only when the work is done at night that the problem of uniform and even lighting arises, and it is a problem that requires expert handling and planning.

Besides the intensity and location of light, it is necessary to pay attention to its colour. It has been uniformly experienced in a large number of cases that light that resembles daylight very nearly is the best and most beneficial one. Hence, white light has been considered the most superior. And in coloured lights, the best is a light yellow but a healthy yellow and not a sickly pale yellow. All other coloured lights harm the eyes to some extent.

12.6.2 Temperature: Temperature of the working premises has considerable and direct influence on the worker's health—it having been found that working in too high or too low temperature leads to disease and accident. Proper temperature maintains good health among workers, and reduces the number of accidents as external conditions do not divert the attention of the worker and thus reduce his efficiency. H.M. Vernon found that in the British mines, when the temperature is about 75° Fahrenheit, there were greater number of accidents since the perception and sensibility of workers were also adversely affected. Extreme temperatures in working areas cause discomfort to the workers, so much so that the quality as well as quantity of his output is reduced. Temperature further influences the ventilation in a room, as it is essential for proper ventilation and flow of air to have only an adequate temperature.

12.6.3 Ventilation: Inflow of fresh air is essential in a place of work, as its absence tends to increase the fatigue and laziness or drowsiness of the workers. Air easily becomes contaminated in places where a large number of individuals work together, such as mines, factories and offices. For this, the use of exhaust fans is particularly desirable. Transport should be freely and easily available in places of work. Health is adversely affected if the percentage of oxygen in air is varied even within very narrow limits. According to Poffenberger, when the percentage of oxygen in air tends to fall, the workers show signs of adverse effect. Ventilation also influences the body temperature of the workers, and if the body temperature varies, it leads to fatigue and drowsiness. Another important factor is the presence as well as the percentage of humidity in the air. Excessive humidity has undeniably a very harmful influence.

12.6.4 Noise: Excessive noise normally distracts attention and obstructs smooth working. It is for this reason that in every industry attention is now being paid to the noise produced, and efforts are made to curb noise that distracts attention. But noise of a continuous nature is often found to be more soothing than disturbing, and when it is discontinued, it disturbs the attention of people used to it. The truth of the matter is that only excessive noise is harmful and has the worst effect on the system. Keeping in mind these observations, efforts should be made to regulate noise.

12.6.5 Hours of Work: Profession in which hours of work are so long and are unhygienically planned that the worker is completely fatigued by the time he stops working and finds himself confronted with the problem of continuously decreasing efficiency. In addition to this, these professions become prey to all kinds of very serious problems of human relationships. When a worker is compelled to work for long hours beyond his physical endurance limits, he becomes diseased and loses his efficiency. Besides, his irritability increases significantly. For this reason, in most progressive nations, the government promulgates certain orders whereby the hours of work for different occupations, for individuals of different ages and of different sexes, are determined. If need for more work arises, the employer is faced either with the alternative of indulging in illegal activity or remunerating the worker for this extra labour. But if he chooses to evade these laws, he incurs the displeasure of the law, and this is never to his advantage.

12.6.6 Rest Pauses: Whenever the ability and endurance of an individual is tested even if he appears to be normal in this respect, he cannot work continuously for a long period of time. After a certain period of time, he feels the need for a rest, and his need has been found to have psychological justification as it has been found that better results can be obtained by working in shifts and periods then by working continuously. An increase of ten to twenty percent in production efficiency has been found to occur as a result of provision of rest in between work. The length and frequency of rest that is required depends upon the nature of work, the endurance and age of the worker and the general conditions of work. Hard work requires relatively longer and greater number of rest pauses. Similarly, women, young children and old require longer and greater number of rest pauses, then young men. Now-a-days, in practically every profession and occupation, rests of 15 minutes to an hour is provided once or more so that the worker may be able to take refreshments and restore his vitality otherwise. Rest in between hours of work not only removes fatigue but also eliminates the element of monotony and boredom, thereby regenerating enthusiasm and validity.

12.6.7 Music: One of the conditions of work taken into consideration is music. From their experiments, W.A. Keir and H.C. Smith concluded that music has a beneficial and desirable influence upon the mental condition of worker, and thus it helps to induce some increase in their productive capacity. And one often sees people singing at their work, a phenomenon particularly obvious in the case of Indian women working at the grinder or in the fields or even when at their domestic chores. The rhythm in music has a beneficial effect on the rate of working. Tata Group in India provides music in their various factories. In Western countries, particularly in the United States, the use of music in factories and other working places is steadily on the increase. Through a questionnaire H.C. Smith collected the views of one thousand workers regarding the provision of music in working places, and found that as many as 98 percent of them were in favour of it, as they found considerable pleasure in it. The influence of music on routine work is as yet under extensive study.

12.6.8 Other Physical Conditions: In addition to these above conditions, they are other physical and material considerations which influence the worker and his work. For example, if there is good and clean provision of urinals, latrines, bathrooms, refreshment rooms, canteen, etc., the worker time in the office becomes more pleasant, and many of his difficulties are removed. A place of work should not be foul smelling, neither should it be dirty or dusty, as any of these conditions disgusts the worker.

12.7 Psychological Conditions of Work

12.7.1 Behaviour of Those in Authority: A worker's mind is very susceptible to the behaviour of his boss. If the behaviour of authorities is desirable and good, the worker's enthusiasm and interest in his work is maintained, but if their behaviour is bad and inconsiderate, it is potentially a dangerous state as it can lead to conflict and unnecessary tension that has the worst effect upon production. Good behaviour does not imply laxity in administration and in dealing with the workers, as in such circumstances it is inevitable that the lazy and designing individuals in the organisation will have a field day and do not work at all. It is essential that constant attention be paid to the worker's performance, but fact and diplomacy should be employed if it becomes necessary to point out his shortcomings. Senior officials and employers who are in the habit of constantly haranguing and bickering with their staff, are very often faced with continuous conflict and non-cooperation. Employees are not inclined to respect and work for people who are irritable, highly inflammable and ingratiating types. Working under a considerate individual not only keeps the worker happy but also inspires him to work more and work better.

12.7.2 Mutual Relations of Workers: One of the psychological conditions of working is the nature of relations that exist between the workers themselves. Where the number of workers is fairly large, and the nature of work demands their constant cooperation, better results are obtained if the workers have happy relations. If the relations are not all that can be desired, work suffers. And particularly work that requires comparative effort is a total loss as there is no cooperation.

12.7.3 Security in Profession: If the worker is confident that he is secured in his job, then his work shows definite improvements. In a profession that offers no security of employment, or in a position in which one can never be confident of remaining safe, a worker cannot work with enthusiasm or with his mind on the work. Hence, a profession must offer security of future employment. After a certain predetermined period of service has been completed, the worker should be made permanent in his position, as is now done in all government jobs and many private firms. Even most government in many countries have made laws regarding such employment procedure. Besides this minimal security of profession, other inducements like insurance during unemployment, old age insurance, and security or insurance in the event of accidents that render the individual incapable of further work are being propagated by companies and governments. Now-a-days, in all progressive states, government and other general employers make provision for these benefits, as in their absence it is only natural for the worker to spend time wondering about his future.

12.7.4 Satisfaction of Life's Needs: Every individual has some personal and other family requirements, such as adequate food and housing for his family, and purchasing power to the extent of his other reasonable needs. Besides this, there are certain needs that foster self respect, and these too cannot be neglected. Progress has made it necessary for employers to pay attention to these aspects of the human personality also. Consequently, they have to initiate and finance certain schemes of labour welfare that involve some expenditure, but which provide many direct and indirect benefits to the worker that places him in a very favourable state of mind. Their needs being fulfilled, they are inclined to respect their employers and work for their better being in turn. They are thus helped in leading a pleasant and contended life, and they bend their back to their work with a will. They have confidence in their employers, and thus they are never induced to work contrary to the interests of their employers.

12.7.5 Incentive in Industry: Motives have an important place in the life of a man. In the absence of a motive, no individual can either work hard or do anything to better his lot in life or improve his work in any way. Inspiration of this kind is available to the individual in his trade in the forms of various kinds of incentives such as increase in wages, praise by authorities, promotion, bonus, etc. Incentives are now an important part of any geared up industry. In most progressive nations, the workers stand to benefit through bonus if the production, and thus the earning of their enterprise, goes up. In most professions, an individual is promoted to a senior position if he shows satisfactory or more than satisfactory work. If the people in authority are sensible people, they will always praise the extra efforts of their subordinates. Their wages can also be increased so as to form an extra inducement.

All the aforementioned physical and psychological conditions have considerable importance for commerce and industry. Psychologists have now seriously drawn the attention of the industrialists to this aspect. It is necessary not only with regard to economic or fiscal gain, but also with regard to humanity that the workers should have an opportunity to work in beneficial conditions, both physical and psychological. Workers being part and parcel of the fibre of the nation, the government should take steps to have such conditions created. When such a system is in existence in industry, the conflicts are materially reduced and the production increases with the results that the employer, the employee and the state, all benefit.

12.8 Fatigue: Types and Causes

Fatigue of workers is an important problem in motivation and industrial psychology. Fatigue is short of negative appetite for activity. It arises due to continuous or late work. Interest in work and quantity of output both decline as fatigue increases. Of course, fatigue may be due to excessive physical or mental demands on employees or due to the nature of working assignments. Whatever the causes are, it is an important motivational problem.

12.8.1 Types of Fatigue: Fatigue can be both mental and physical—their description is as follows:

A. Physical Fatigue: In physical fatigue, as is evident from the name itself, one finds physical characteristics of fatigue. Physical efficiency and capacity fall down and physical coordination becomes difficult. A poisonous fluid known as lactic acid is produced in the muscles and the nervous system, and when this increases beyond a certain level the entire body becomes lax.

If it is confined to any one part of the body, then that particular part becomes tired but when exhaustion increases it is introduced into the blood stream and steadily spreads over the entire body. In addition to lactic acid, the body also produces ammonia and carbon dioxide during fatigue. Both these elements are poisonous and by their influence, the energizing elements in the body steadily decline while the poisonous matter increases.

Many psychologists have examined the condition of fatigue, the most valuable work having been done by Miller, Helmholtz and Wundt. Miller confined his study to the state of the nerves in a condition of fatigue. Later on, Helmholtz made a study of the function of the sensory nerves and motor nerves and discovered that in a condition of fatigue, the experience of anything is conveyed to the brain in greater time while the motor nerves take a longer time to react than under normal conditions. Helmholtz invented the Myograph, an instrument used to measure the contraction of muscles. It was later used in 1858 by Wundt in his experiments. This instrument is now used to measure fatigue.

B. Mental Fatigue: Fatigue is not merely physical because it is sometimes manifested even when one has done no physical work. This is called mental fatigue. Mental fatigue is normally apparent after excessive physical fatigue. The symptoms of mental fatigue include absence of desire to work, emotional condition, lack of interest and concentration, lack of normal efficiency in work, desire to rest, etc. At times, one's efficiency does not suffer despite some mental fatigue but this is a rare case. One example of mental fatigue is boredom in which one experiences mental fatigue because one's energy has not been properly consumed. One important cause of mental fatigue is the absence of motivation and of a proper aptitude. In such a case, an individual loses interest in his work even though he is not physically exhausted. People complain of fatigue despite good working conditions—their aptitude is not correct and there is absence of sufficient motivation.

12.8.2 Causes of Fatigue: In different professions, there are different causes which lead to fatigue. Important causes can be briefly summarised as under.

A. Long Hours of Work: In some industries, the hours of work are so long that the workers become exhausted while in fact these longer hours of work do not result in a proportionate increase in production. Many researches have thrown light on this fact. Muscio has mentioned the case of one lady worker who worked only six hours instead of the conventional twelve hours a day observed by the other workers and still showed a higher level of production than any other worker. In this factory, the working hours were from six to eight in the morning, eight thirty to twelve thirty; one thirty to five thirty; and from eight thirty to twelve thirty. This particular lady, refused to work before breakfast and late at night, explaining that by working for such a long time she could not maintain her efficiency. Over a period of one month, it was seen that she worked for 150 hours as compared to the other workers who worked for 237 hours, despite which she showed more output than the others. It is evident from the research conducted in various countries on the methods of work, that production is higher in shorter working week than in longer working weeks.

B. Absence of Rest Periods: If a person works for a long time continuously then he feels fatigued. If he does not take rest and continues to work, then his fatigue increases even more rapidly because he is working in an exhausted condition. If he is allowed to rest as soon as he begins feeling exhausted, then he returns to his work refreshed and his fatigue does not increase. Hence, it is seen that fatigue is eliminated in all working methods where the workers are allowed to rest for short periods during their working hours because during the period of rest, they can regain their energy. Absence to rest period is an occupational condition which promotes fatigue. Even if some workers steal a few minutes of rest where it is not officially provided for, they do not feel relaxed and rested because during that period their aptitude is not correct. In fact, relaxation of this kind results in greater fatigue. Gillbreath's experiments successfully established that production can be increased by providing periods of rest for the workers instead of keeping them at work continuously.

C. Incorrect Temperature: Incorrect room temperature in another occupational condition which results in fatigue because in these cases, the room is either too hot or too cold. In both cases, the mental and physical conditions of the workers deteriorate and they soon feel exhausted.

D. Absence of Proper Ventilation: If a person does not get clean air where he is working, he soon gets tired. In an office or factory in which the air is polluted, the incidence of fatigue will be far greater than in any other factory where there is adequate ventilation.

E. Improper Illumination: Fatigue also increases if the illumination in the working area is not adequate and proper because the eyes begin to feel exhausted and dry if the light is not enough or too bright. Hence, it is desirable that there should be proper arrangement for illumination in factories and offices—proper lighting from the right direction. For example, when working, it is desirable that the light source should be placed behind and to the left of the worker. If this is not done, then the eyes suffer great strain. While working on a machine, it is desirable that those instruments should be lighted up which are to be seen constantly by the operator. Hence, the light provided should neither be too little nor too much, for in both these conditions, the strain on the eyes leads to fatigue.

F. Design of the Machinery: Certain machines are so designed that they tend to exhaust and tire the operator working on them. Hence, modern psychologists have given suggestions even in the construction of machines so that they should be so designed so as to minimize fatigue and increase production. This branch of industrial psychology involves the least possible amount of movement while maintaining the highest level of production. When the workers become used to operating such a machine, their fatigue is reduced and their work improves.

G. Absence of Adequate Seat: It is a well known fact that a person feels exhausted much earlier if he has to operate a machine while standing. That is why the absence of an adequate seat is one occupational condition which causes fatigue. Another important feature of the seat is that it should not offer too much comfort because in that case, the operator feels sleepy. On the other hand, it should not be so hard that the operator may face discomfort. Arrangement for a proper seat can help in reducing fatigue.

H. Excessive Noise: Another occupational condition which increases fatigue is the presence of excessive noise at place of work. An individual can work for a long time in an atmosphere which is peaceful and free of noise. Some degree of noise can be tolerated, for it has no appreciable effect on work but when noise rises above a certain level, it creates fatigue. Now experiments are being made to find out if the noise produced by the machinery is high enough in pitch to induce fatigue. If this happens, then efforts are made to reduce the pitch of sound produced and hence reduce the level of noise. Karnhouser conducted an experiment for the typists who worked in a noisy environment for four days. The psychologist came to the conclusion that their work went down by 3.2 percent while the incidence of errors went up by 23 percent. In an experiment conducted for Western workers engaged in stitching showed 7.5 percent more production when working in peaceful surroundings than when working in a noisy environment.

I. Unhealthy Conditions: Fatigue is intimately connected with health. The occupational conditions are such that they do not promote good health and they are also conductive to fatigue. Unhealthy conditions include such factors as incorrect room temperature, improper ventilation, excessive noise, etc. In addition to these, certain other occupational conditions like excessively humidity, absence of rest, presence of some disturbing smell, inadequate arrangement for medicine and medical attendance or the total lack of such facilities also have a bad influence upon the health of the workers with the result that they soon become tired.

J. Absence of Proper Training: In every profession, there are certain functions which require some training before they can be properly performed. If such functions are entrusted to untrained employees then these workers become exhausted very rapidly. Hence, the employees should be trained by the best methods about the easiest and least training way of handling certain instruments. They should also be guided in adjusting the hours of work and the periods of rest according to their individual differences. Hence, the absence of proper training is also an occupational condition which results in fatigue.

K. Lack of Sleep: In factories in which the workers have to work at night and cannot get adequate rest during the day, lack of sleep forms another factor which results in fatigue. To eliminate this, facilities for sleep should be provided for the workers so that they can sleep and take rest. Absence of sleep is invariably an exhausting factor, irrespective of the condition which leads to it.

L. Low Morale: Conditions which are conductive to low morale are also conducive to fatigue. Conditions which result in low morale and harmful attitudes towards the management, hatred, suspicion and jealousy, dissatisfaction with work and absence of any hope, mental unrest and dissatisfaction, uninteresting work, improper rules governing promotions, absence of a proper wage increase, improper methods of distribution of wages, lack of adjustment on the part of management, etc. In all such conditions, fatigue also increases rapidly and leads to physical fatigue. Conditions in which high morale can be generated also leads to energetic work for which effort are made to make the social atmosphere cooperative and refreshing or encouraging. This must be done so that the worker can work for a long time without feeling exhausted.

12.8.3 Reducing the Fatigue: The chief method of reducing fatigue is to eliminate all occupational conditions which increase it. Hence, mention will here be made of the means by which fatigue can be reduced. It should always be kept in mind that work invariably results in some degree of exhaustion and that there can be no ways of eliminating fatigue completely. One can only hope to devise means by which fatigue can be reduced or controlled before it becomes excessive. Briefly, this can be done in the following ways.

A. Reducing the Hours of Work: One way of reducing fatigue is to reduce the hours of work. It has been seen in many experiments that fatigue is reduced when working hours are reduced, whereas the production does not fall proportionately and in many cases it actually increases. In 1928, Sheppard pointed out that for the previous thirty years, workers were made to work ten hours a day for six days a week in all American industries. On the other hand, the workers are now made to work eight hours, and on Saturdays, they are required to work only four hours, while Sunday is a day for rest. But actually production has increased as a result of this decrease in the hours of work.

Many other experiments have substantiated Sheppard's conclusions. Hence, one way of reducing fatigue is to reduce the hours of work. But at the same time, care should be taken to avoid reducing working hours to such an extent that the worker's energy is not fully utilized. The most appropriate method is to have sufficient working hours in which the worker can continue to work without feeling totally exhausted. Evidently, the working hours will differ from industry to industry, according to the nature of the work.

B. Provision of Rest Periods: Another way of reducing fatigue is to introduce properly timed periods of rest. An appropriate period of rest involves calculation of the total rest period allowed in proportion to the work expected from the worker. And a properly timed rest period implies the time at which this rest should be allowed and the frequency with which it should be allowed. Many experiments on this subject have yielded a fund of valuable facts. According to Vernon, the worker should be allowed rest after every hour while according to Sheppard, the worker who works for eight hours a day should be allowed to rest for 16 percent of the total working time. It is evident that in providing rest periods, one must consider the total rest period in proportion to the working hours as well as the frequency and duration for which it should be given.

C. Proper Ventilation: Fatigue can also be reduced by improving the ventilation so that the polluted air is eliminated and fresh air is admitted into the factory. Most factories make use of exhaust fans designed to suck the polluted air out of a room or a hall.

D. Arrangement for Proper Lighting: Fatigue can also be reduced to some extent if proper provision is made for lighting up the area in which the workers work. For this, it is necessary that the light should come from the right direction and should be of a particular intensity. The advantage in this is that the eyes do not suffer strain and hence the workers do not become tired quickly.

E. Improvements in the Design of Machines: The share and the size of the machine operated by the worker also influence fatigue. If the machine is so designed that it can be run efficiency by making the minimum possible movements, the worker will not feel exhausted.

F. Proper Seating Arrangement: A proper seating arrangement for the worker also helps to reduce fatigue. As far as possible, the workers should be allowed to work while sitting. The seat should provide normal comfort to avoid fatigue but it should not be too comfortable for in that case it will induce sleep. But it should also not be too hard.

G. Control over the Noise: Since excessive noise also induces fatigue, it is desirable to have some control over the amount of noise in or near the working place, if fatigue is to be avoided. This can be done in many ways. It is more difficult to reduce the noise made by the machines installed in the factories but efforts should be made to control the noise produced. If the noise in the factory or office is less, the workers fatigue will also be less.

H. Arrangements for Industrial or Professional Training: The worker feels less fatigue in manipulating a machine for which he has been trained because he does not make any necessary movements. Hence, professional training can also help to reduce fatigue.

I. Proper Arrangements for Sleep: In many kinds of work, it is necessary to provide some arrangement for sleep. Even if the worker is given a chance to sleep on a comfortable bed for only half an hour out of the total working time, much of his fatigue disappears. Such an arrangement is particularly useful for the workers working in night shifts.

J. High Morale: High morale can also help to reduce fatigue among the workers. Maintenance of high morale requires an attitude favourable towards the management, self-generated discipline, group administration, enthusiasm, mental satisfaction and peace, respect for and confidence in the management, etc. If these factors are present, the incidence of fatigue is much lower.

12.8.4 Criteria of Fatigue: The criteria for fatigue implies the symptoms by which its presence can be diagnosed and recognised in order to understand that it is essential to keep in mind the various aspects of fatigue. Since fatigue is a psycho-physical condition, its symptoms are both mental and physical. It can be recognised by the following factors.

A. Feeling of Exhaustion: The chief symptom of fatigue is the feeling of fatigue even if the individual is not feeling physically exhausted. In a state of exhaustion, the desire of work is noticeably reduced and the desire to rest is clearly heightened. Generally, it also leads to a fall in an individual's production, though this is not universally true. In the state of exhaustion, the individuals feeling about work change evinces no desire to do any kind of work.

B. Muscular Condition: In a state of fatigue, the muscles lose their power to contract and expand. Hence, psychologically, fatigue is muscular condition and the fatigue of the muscles to contract and expand is one criterion of fatigue.

C. Chemical Changes: As a person works, the production of acetic acid and other poisonous chemicals in his body increases. In a healthy body, the oxygen is properly distributed through the blood stream with the result that poisonous matter is eliminated from the body. When the muscles become tired, this process of elimination does not work sufficiently. This leads to a fall in the quantity of glycogen in the body along with an increase in the quantity of poisonous matter. In this manner, many chemical changes occur in the body during fatigue, and it can be recognised by these chemical changes.

D. Nervous Slackness: One criterion of mental exhaustion is nervous slackness. Sometimes it is caused by muscular fatigue but it also has many other causes. In a state of nervous exhaustion, the nerves lose their power to react with the result that the individual cannot work efficiently. Many experiments have established that, in a condition of exhaustion, the nerves and muscles do not have the power to react properly or to achieve the normal state of excitation. As a result of this slackness, the sense organs do not react properly. The sense of smell is particularly influenced while the powers of seeing, hearing and touching are also adversely influenced.

E. Change in the Mental Condition: One criterion of fatigue is the change in the mental condition because in an exhausted condition, an individual experiences deterioration of his menial powers and a loss of interest. He cannot concentrate upon anything for a long time and becomes bored with work. Because of his influence upon the mind, fatigue is considered a psycho-physical phenomenon.

F. Increase in the Number of Accidents: An analysis of accidents in industry has revealed that a majority of accidents occur either in the morning or late in the evening. This fact has been generally substantiated by studies in Germany, England and America. A study of fatigue has also shown that it is the greatest early in the morning and late in the evening. Hence, one can estimate the extent of industrial fatigue from the number of accidents. For these reasons, now provisions have been made for introducing rest periods in the early hours and in the late evenings. This pattern of accidents can be seen in almost any industry but while the morning accidents are uniformly present, the late evening accidents follow various patterns in different industries. Accidents in the late evening take place more rapidly but the total number is not much more than that of accidents in the morning. One can see a difference in the number of accidents that take place during the morning and the night shifts. Hence, the relationship between fatigue and accidents is obvious.

It should be kept in mind that despite the clear relationship between fatigue and accidents, fatigue is not the sole cause of accidents and for this reason an increase in accidents is not a criterion of increasing fatigue. Many other factors apart from fatigue often prove more important in causing accidents. For example, women are more accident prone than men because women tend to tire easily and more rapidly. It cannot be denied that in a state of exhaustion, individuals become restless and cannot control their movements properly. They may even go to sleep but lack concentration. Despite this, fatigue cannot be accepted as a cause of accidents.

G. Fall in Production: Sometimes fatigue is defined in terms of the fall in production. As has already been mentioned, in connecting with accidents, the early morning shift and the late evening shift result in accidents and also in a fall in production. The cause of this fall in production is believed to be fatigue because as fatigue increases, the efficiency of the worker decreases. During the first hour in the morning, the production rate rises steeply because this is the warming up period. The warming up can be due to numerous mental and physical causes. And the period consumed in warming up to one's work will depend as much upon the work as upon the individual differences between one worker and another.

Two factors which are responsible for the rate of the

worker's performance are the worker's health and the nature of the conditions under which he has to work. It is normally seen that production reaches its highest peak in the third hour after which production again begins to fall due to fatigue. It is for this reason that rest period is provided after the third hour of work. In addition to the above factors, all other symptoms of physical and mental fatigue can be accepted as the criteria of fatigue. Fatigue can be recognised by such mental and physical conditions as change in respiration, blood circulation, blood pressure, disinterest, lack of concentration, slackness, etc. Nowadays, many scientific instruments are also used to measure fatigue.

12.9 Monotony

Monotony is also a mental condition that is reflected in labour output. Monotonous operations (or rather operations that appear to the individual employees as monotonous) tend to result in shifts of interest, with intervals of disinterest and day dreaming. Monotony is not characteristic of work rather it is an impact of work and the mental condition of a worker. The major causes leading to monotony may include the routine nature of work, to repeat the same work part, lack of change in work, lack of variety in movements, etc. Sometimes, the purpose of the work also makes a work monotonous. If the worker does not think the work as useful and positive, we will feel monotony and boredom in that work. Excessive division of work, mechanisation of operations, lack of human relations have also contributed to the problem of monotony.

12.9.1 Measures to Remove Monotony: The following steps are useful to remove monotony.

A. Job Enlargement: Job enlargement involves a horizontal loading or expansion or the adding of more tasks of the same general nature or type. It provides the necessary change for the worker and he does not feel boredom and monotony in the work.

B. Job Enrichment: It is an extension of job enlargement. The difference between job enrichment and job enlargement lies on the nature of addition to the job. Job enrichment involves vertical loading giving additional challenges. Thus, it applies to improvement of job in such a way that it has more wide dimensions, more opportunities for achievement, recognition, responsibility, achievement and growth.

C. Job Rotation: Job rotation involves the change in work and work place. If possible, job rotation should also be applied in order to overcome monotony.

D. Provision of Music: The provision of music also makes the work interesting and pleasing. The researches have proved the utility of music in routine types of jobs.

E. Employee Counselling: Employee counselling is also an important method of overcoming monotony in work. The opportunity of counselling makes the workers interested in work, keeps him involved in it and change the attitude of the workers towards the work.

13

Motivation, Morale and Job Satisfaction

The primary task of a manager is that of maintaining an organisation that functions effectively. To do so, he must see that his subordinates work efficiently and produce results that are beneficial to the organisation. Organisational goals can never be achieved without subordinate's willingness to put their best efforts.

Here arises the problem of motivation, 'the capacity of work' and 'willingness to work', which are two different things. A man can be physically, mentally and technically fit to work but he may not be willing to work. Hence, the need for motivation. Motivating a worker is to create a need and a desire on the part of a worker to better his present performance. Thus, performance is determined by two factors, viz. level of ability to do certain work and level of motivation. This can be expressed as follows:

Performance = Ability x Motivation.

13.1 Meaning of Motivation

'Motivation' is a term derived from the word 'motive'. We can define 'motive' as something which makes a person active in a particular way. It is an inner impulse causing man to act. A person works to satisfy his needs. Hence, human needs are the cause of action and motivation is a process of causing the man to realise these needs. Following are some important definitions of motivation.

"Motivation is the act of stimulating someone of oneself to get a desired course of action, without pushing the right button to get desired results"-Michel J. Jucius

"Motivation can be defined as a willingness to expand energy to achieve a good or rewards"-Dale Beach

"Motivation refers to the way in which urges, derives, desires, aspirations, strivings or needs directly control or explain the behaviour of human beings"-McFarland

"Motivation means a process of stimulating people to action to accomplish the desired goals"-W.G. Scot

Thus, it is clear from these definitions that different experts have defined motivation in their own words. However, the basic contents are the same. On the analysis of these definitions, we can derive the following characteristics of motivation:

1. Motivation is a psychological phenomenon which generates within an individual. Needs are feelings in the mind of a person that lacks certain thing. Such feelings affect the behaviour of the person.
2. Each individual in the organisation is a self-contained and inseparable unit and all his needs are inter-related. These affect the behaviour in different ways. Moreover, feeling of needs is a continuous process, as such these create continuity in human behaviour.
3. Motivation is the product of anticipated values from an action and the perceived probability and these values will be achieved by the action. The anticipated value is called 'value' and it is defined as the strength of a person's preference for one outcome in relation to others. The perceived probability is called 'expectancy' and it is defined as the strength of belief that a particular act will be followed by a particular outcome. Thus, motivational relationship can be expressed by the formula:

   Motivation = Valence x Expectancy

13.2 Types of Motivation

Motivation can be positive or negative. Punishments, reprimands, fear or loss of job are methods where people work in fear. On the other hand, positive motivation, sometimes called 'anxiety' reducing motivation or the 'correct approach', offers something valuable to the person (pay, praise appreciation, etc.) for acceptable performance. Motivation can be classified as internal or external motivation also.

Why do people work? It is a fundamental question to be answered before preparing any plan for motivation. It is the intensity of human wants which motivates people to work. Employee motivation gets support and nourishment from the satisfaction of human wants. To increase an individual's work effectiveness, motivation aims at providing all sorts of stimulus and incentive to employees at work or at home. As incentives increase the intensity and duration of human efforts, motivation seeks to bring into operation the full play of such incentives. Incentives may be either be economic or non-economic. Hawthorne's experiments have demonstrated that non-economic incentives are more impressive than financial incentives.

13.3 Importance of Motivation

Motivation is an important function of management. Explaining the importance of motivation E.F.L. Breach writes, "*The problem of motivation is the key to management actions and in its executive form; it is among the chief tasks of the general manager. We may safely lay it down that the tone of an organisation is a reflection of the motivation from the top*". Motivation is getting the members of the team to pull weight effectively, to give their loyalty to the group and organisation, to carry out properly the activities allocated and generally to play an efficient part in the purpose or task that the organisation has undertaken. Motivated employees are the real assets of an organisation.

Technology, system and methods become ineffective when people lose zeal and enthusiasm for work. All administrative actions lose their relevance unless the members of the enterprise are willing to contribute their efforts for the fulfilment of their assigned tasks. The main function of management is to develop and increase a desire in every member of the organisation to work effectively in his position. This overall improves the morale of the employees. Good motivational measures result in increased productivity. It fosters the cooperative spirit among the subordinates and their satisfaction level also goes high. In a nutshell, to achieve organisational and individual goals in an economic and efficient manner, motivation is an important tool in the hands of management to direct the behaviour of subordinates in the desired and appropriate direction and thus minimize the waste of human and other resources.

The importance of motivation in an organisation can be summed up as follows.

13.3.1 High Performance Level: Motivated employees put higher performance as compared to other employees. The high performance is a must for an organisation and motivation is a vital requirement for high performance. A number of researches have proved the relationship between high performance and high motivation.

13.3.2 Low Employee Turnover and Absenteeism: A motivated employee says in the organisation more and their absenteeism is quite low. High turnover and absenteeism create many problems in the organisation. Recruiting, training and development of large number of new personnel does not take long time but it is extensive too. In a competitive economy, this is almost an impossible task. Moreover, this also affects the reputation of the firm adversely. Motivation brings these rates lower.

13.3.3 Acceptance of Organisational Changes: The changes in organisation are a usual phenomenon due to various reasons such as changes in technology, value system, etc. Organisation has to cope with these changes to cope up with the requirement of time. When the changes are introduced in the organisation, there is a tendency to resist them. However, if the employees are properly motivated, they accept these changes with zeal and enthusiasm and support in their proper implementation too.

13.4 Techniques or Methods for Motivation

Since human motives governing human behaviour and

attitude towards work are multiple, management can employ a variety of techniques to motivate the staff. Some important techniques are as follows.

- **Monetary Techniques:** These techniques are based on this popular brief that a man works for money. Hence, an attraction of getting more money will prove to be the most powerful motivator. Incentives like more pay (through various premium plans), fringe benefits, security of tenure, conditions of service, etc. are some examples of the monetary techniques motivation.
- **Job based Techniques:** These techniques are based on social, human and psychological beliefs. Job simplification, job rotation, job enlargement, job enrichment, freedom in planning for work, sense of recognition, responsibility and achievement are some examples of such techniques.
- **MBO Technique:** Peter Drucker, a well known author of management, has developed this technique which emphasizes on self control and self motivation. It is a participatory technique of motivation whereby managers and their subordinates jointly participate in achieving the common goals. It requires an emphasis on management by objectives policy in the concern.
- **Leadership Styles:** Leadership styles or supervisory techniques also have a great role in motivation of employees. Autocratic, democratic, and free-rein techniques of leadership are important styles and they have their own implications for employee motivation, morale and productivity. The management must try different supervisory styles in different circumstances for different employees.
- **Group Based Techniques:** Herber Bonner a well-known author, has advocated group based techniques for motivating the employees According to him, "Motivation is not wholly, nor even primarily, an individual variable. Certainly its force and direction are functions of the social situation in which it arises and is exercised". Hence, management should foster group consciousness and

cohesiveness among individual employees by laying down general norms and guidelines of work for the group as a whole.

- **Sensitivity Training:** This is a technique of training given to groups of managers (known as T-groups) themselves so that they behave with and motivate their subordinates better. The sensitivity training is imparted to make the managers understand themselves better, becoming more open-minded, developing insight into group process, and cultivating a systematic approach towards the problem of motivation. A manager thus trained is supposed to be more consistently able and willing to communicate with his subordinates and inspire them to contribute their best to the common goals and objectives.

Though motivation is an important task of management, but it is a part of process of management. It should not be overlooked by the management. Management should have a balanced approach in this respect. Further, there cannot be a single source of motivation, a system of motivation is required—a coordinated set of incentives, positive as well as negative, available for selective application to elicit the best efforts of individuals. Hence, a coordinated approach is required in this direction.

13.5 Problems in Motivation

Motivation is mainly a psychological and social problem. Its concepts in theory are very clear while its practice in actual life is very difficult. The motivation of employees involves the following problems:

- **Problem of Implementation:** First problem in motivation is of implementation. It involves the decision as regards to deciding what should to be done to motivate one individual. People differ in their expectations hence they require separate types of incentives to be motivated.
- **Problem of Moderate Motivation:** The motivators should keep this fundamental thing in mind that

motivation is an important tool in the hand of management to direct the behaviour of subordinates in the desired direction but it has its own limitations also. Subordinates can be motivated to a limited extent only.

- **Problems of Uneven Motivation:** The problem of uneven motivation is also important. An executive should know the individual characteristics which determine the effectiveness of motivational measures to a large extent. All individuals do not possess equal education, like attitudes, and level of aspirations. Educated and skilled employees can be motivated more in comparison to unskilled and uneducated workers. The basis of motivation is the need of employees. They should be recognised, identified and then satisfied through various types of incentives.
- **Limitations of Employees:** The management should keep in mind the limitations of employees also. They are not only for business organisations. They owe certain responsibilities for their families, social circle, city and nation also. Hence, the management should not expect their whole hearted loyalty and dedication for organisation only.
- **Motivation is Situation Oriented:** Implementing the concept of motivation is always situation oriented. The management should try to understand the situation properly and then any measure should be taken to motivate the employees. To motivate others, the executive himself must be well motivated. He will prove to be an example to be emulated. Subordinates get inspiration from him.
- **Motivation is an Internal Instinct:** In the last but not the least, the management should not forget that motivation by nature is an internalised process. It comes from inside but some reinforcements are needed to utilize it for practical purposes. Manager can give only start but actual and effective motivation will depend upon the internal will of the subordinate itself.

13.6 Classification and Hierarchy of Needs

The central problem of motivation, as far as the management of an organisation is concerned, is how to induce a group of people to work. A manager before planning for motivation should invariably know why people do the work. The ability to make effective motivational decisions requires knowledge about the motives which bring about purposeful behaviour. Motivation has its roots in such motives within a person which induce him to behave in a particular manner. These motives are known as 'wants', 'needs', or 'fears', etc. These are the drivers for work. They are the initiating and sustaining forces of behaviour. They have a direct influence on an individual, since they determine his thoughts and actions. A person's needs, working in conjunction with his emotions and other psychological functions act as a motive that dictates his actions and behaviour. What an individual perceives as the real world about him, how he feels, what old thought patterns come into play, his current activities, all these processes and many more are influenced by his needs and the means he uses to satisfy them.

13.6.1 Types of Needs: There are various ways to classify needs. A simple one is the classification of needs as: (i) basic, physiological, primary or lower order needs, and (ii) social or psychological needs, secondary, higher order, or derived needs.

1. **Physiological Needs:** These are animal drives which are essential for survival. These needs are common to all human beings, though their intensity may differ. Some of the physiological needs are food, sex, air to breathe, satisfactory temperature, etc. These needs arise out of the basic physiology of life and are important for survival and preservation of species. These needs are also conditioned by social practices. According to the concept of economic man, these are the only wants of a human being and he attempts to satisfy them only. But researches in human behaviour show that psychological needs are rather equally

more important for human beings.

2. **Social-Psychological Needs:** These needs are most nebulous because they represent needs of the mind and spirit, rather than of physical body. They are also vague. These are learnt through experience and environment and as such they are also called learned or derived needs. Examples are rivalry, self esteem, sense of duty belonging, etc. A person's real secondary needs are often hidden so that even he cannot recognise them. They also change according to time and circumstances. These may further be classified as:

- Social needs which are related to get a high position and status in the society or to get praise from others.
- Ego needs which are related with a person's self ego. These may further be classified into two parts, viz.: (i) those needs that relate to one's self esteem—needs of self-confidence, achievement, competence and knowledge, and (ii) those needs that relate to one's reputation—needs for status, recognition, appreciation, etc.

Niles has classified the various needs as needs for security, achievement, recognition, sense of belongingness, monetary and opportunity for progress and worth. According to her, needs are the basic factors in motivation.

A.H. Maslow has given certain priority to needs and has classified various needs as basic physiological needs like safety and security, belonging and social activity, esteem and status, and self-realisation and fulfilment.

13.6.2 Non-fulfilment of Needs: When a need is felt, a person tries to get it satisfied resulting in a particular behaviour (desired one). However, because of some reasons if the need is not satisfied, the person becomes frustrated. The person would try to modify his behaviour to eliminate factors responsible for non-fulfilment of his need. However, the things blocking the person in achieving his goal are numerous and many of them may be beyond his control. He fails to control these factors and frustration remains there. Its main utility is this that it has suggested the priority and nature of needs. This hierarchical concept of needs is important for understanding the managerial task in relation of human resources working in organisations. His approach was direct, simple and practical. Maslow has himself pointed out that this hierarchy of needs is not rigid and fixed in order and it is not the same for all individuals. Individuals who are high in position in organisations are able to satisfy their higher order needs but the lower level people are unable to do so. Once an individual has moved from a lower level of needs to a higher level of needs, the lower level needs assume a less important role.

Apart from the merits of this theory, Maslow's theory of human needs has certain weakness too. First, it is a general expression and not a specific one. Secondly, the levels in the hierarchy are not rigidly fixed. The boundaries between them are hazy and overlapping. Thirdly, it does not have any allowance for exceptions. Fourthly, this approach overlooks the inner-action of needs. An act is seldom motivated by a single need. Any act is more likely to be caused by several needs. These limitations should be kept in mind by the management when preparing any plan for motivation. Again people differ in their expectations significantly. The same need does not lead to the same response in all individuals Hence a diversity in motivational efforts is also required.

13.7 Herzberg's Theory of Motivation

Needs priority, to a great extent, characterises the types of behaviour. It will be either directed towards achieving certain desirable positive goals, or conversely, towards avoiding other undesirable, negative consequences. Thus, a question may arise as to what variables are perceived to be desirable goals to achieve, and conversely, undesirable conditions to avoid. In this connection, a research study was conducted by Frederick Herzberg of Caste Western Reserve University and associates. This study consisted of an intensive analysis of the experiences and feelings of 200 engineers and accountants in nine different companies in Pittsburgh area of US. During the structured interview, they were asked to describe a few previous job experiences in which they felt 'exceptionally good' or 'exceptionally bad' about jobs. They were also asked to rate the degree of which their feelings were influenced—for better or worse—by each experience by which they described.

In concluding the information from the interview, Herzberg concluded that there were two categories of needs essentially independent of each other, affecting behaviour in different ways. His findings were that there are some job conditions which operate primarily to dissatisfy employees—when the conditions are absent, their presence does not motivate them in a strong way. Another set of job conditions operate primarily to build strong motivation and high job satisfaction, but their absence rarely proves strongly dissatisfying. The first set of job conditions is referred to as maintenance or hygiene factors and second set of job conditions as motivational factors.

13.7.1 Hygiene Factors: According to Herzberg, there are ten maintenance or hygiene factors. These include company policy and administration, technical supervision, inter-personal relationship with supervisors, inter-personal relationship with peers, inter-personal relationship with subordinates, salary, job security, personal life, working conditions and status. These are not an intrinsic part of the job, but they are related to conditions under which a job is performed. They produce no growth in a worker's output; they only prevent losses in worker's performance due to work restrictions. These maintenance factors are necessary to maintain a reasonable level of satisfaction in employees. Any increase beyond this level will not provide any satisfaction to the employees; however, any cut below this level will dissatisfy them. As such, these are also called as dissatisfiers. Since, any increase in these factors will not affect employee's level of satisfaction, these are of no use in motivating them.

13.7.2 Motivational Factors: These factors are capable of having a positive effect on job satisfaction, often resulting in an increase in one's total output. Herzberg includes six factors that motivate employees. These are achievement, recognition, advancement, work itself, possibility of growth and responsibility. Most of these factors are related with job contents. An increase in these factors will satisfy the employees; however, any decrease will not affect their level of satisfaction. Since, they increase the satisfaction of the employees, these can be used in motivating them for higher output.

Herzberg maintains the potency of various factors which is not entirely a function of factors themselves. It is also influenced by the personality characteristics of the individuals. From this point of view, individuals may be classified into two categories—motivation seekers and maintenance seekers. The motivation seekers generally are individuals who are primarily motivated by the 'satisfiers' such as advancement, achievement and other factors associated with work itself. On the other hand, the maintenance seekers tend to be more concerned with factors surrounding the job such as supervision, working conditions, pay, etc.

13.8 Critical Analysis of the Theory

There are many related studies which support the view of Herzberg. The study of a group of supervisors' in utility industry substantially confirms the finding of Herzberg. Another study of scientists, engineers, manufacturing supervisors, hourly technicians and female assemblers' tends to confirm the results and theories from Herzberg's study. It should be added here that in this study, there are differences among the various groups of individuals (scientists, techniques, etc.) about the relative importance of various satisfiers and dissatisfiers. Ishwar Dayal and Saiyadin have analysed the validity of Herzberg's theory. Their research finding of a study in the Indian context are highly supportive of Herzberg's motivation-hygiene theory.

There are various studies, on the other hand, the results of which are against the model given by Herzberg. In a study, it has been found that women employees perceive informal relationship with their fellow employees as motivational factor. Other studies show that motivation and maintenance factors are positively related with job satisfaction and many of the factors which are predominantly maintenance factors are considered motivational factors by lower level employees.

In India also, various such studies have been conducted. These, however, do not correspond with the research findings of Herzberg. In the study by Sawlapurkar of middle level managers, it was found that for the managers some of the maintenance factors such as job security, boss, company, working conditions, etc., were satisfiers and motivating factors. In the study by Lahiri and Srivastava of middle level managers, responsibility, domestic life, accomplishment, job and the utilisation of abilities on the job were found to be motivational factors whereas organisational policy and administration, promotion, salary, superiority and growth were dissatisfiers. In India, more importance is attached to job security because of the fact that job opportunities are limited here considering the number of job aspirants.

Besides, the research studies confronting the two factors satisfiers and dissatisfiers, many writers and thinkers on the subject have argued against the theory as follows.

- In fact, job satisfaction and dissatisfaction are two opposite points on a single continuum. Individuals on the job are affected by the change either in the job environment or in the job content.
- Herzberg's model is 'method bound', and a number of other methods used for similar study have shown different results not supporting his contentions. Thus, the theory has limitations in general acceptability.
- This theory does not attach much importance to pay, status, or interpersonal relationships which are held generally as important contents of satisfaction.

In spite of this criticism, Herzberg's model has been applied in the industry and has provided several new insights. One of these insights is the job enrichment. The job enrichment applies to improvement of jobs in such a way that they have more motivators than before. The idea behind job enrichment is to keep maintenance factors constant or higher while increasing motivational factors. Job enrichment is different from job enlargement practised earlier to make job more attractive. In job enlargement, the basic idea is to change the job to become more complicated and varied so that monotony goes off, while job enrichment seeks to bring more motivators—the job attaching more responsibility, more intrinsically satisfying work conditions and more power over the environment. Thus, Herzberg's model has solved the problems of managers who were wondering why their fancy personnel policies failed to motivate their employees adequately.

13.9 Comparison of Herzberg and Maslow Models

When Herzberg and Maslow models are compared, it can be seen that both the models focus their attention on the relationship i.e. what motivates an individual. Maslow has given it in terms of need hierarchy and has suggested how people try to comparatively meet higher level needs. Thus, any satisfied need can become a motivating factor for the individual and govern his behaviour in that direction. In comparatively socially and economically advanced countries, most of the lower order needs are fulfilled and for people, only higher level needs remain as motivating factors. This is what Herzberg has suggested. Most of his maintenance factors come under comparatively lower order needs. Most of these needs remain satisfied.

However, there is a particular difference between the two models. Maslow emphasises that any unsatisfied need whether of lower order or higher order will motivate individuals. Thus, it has universality in its applicability. It can be applied to lower level workers as well as higher level managers. In underdeveloped countries, where because of lack of socio-economic progress, even lower order needs are not reasonably satisfied, such needs are motivating factors. According to Herzberg, these are hygiene factors and fail to motivate workers.

13.10 Important Elements of a Sound Motivational System

A critical analysis of the various motivational models reveals that there is wide scope of variability in the factors of motivation. As such, management will be in a dilemma as to how to motivate their employees to get best results. Moreover, these models have been given by foreign contributors which are more applicable to their industrial system. In our country, because of different socio-economic conditions, these models are applicable with certain reservations. Thus, while adopting a motivational model, some important considerations should be kept in mind. These can be summarised as follows:

- **Adequate Motivation:** The motivation system should be adequate, covering the entire human force in the organisation and it should cover entire activities of the working force. Sometimes, the presence of a motivational factor fails to produce any effective result, particularly when its amount is too small. In such a case, its energetic force should he increased so that it motivates strongly.
- **Analysis of Motives:** A good motivation system also attempts at analysing the factors which motivate the employees in the prevailing organisational environment. Study of the various needs of the employees, degree of intensity and the prospective consequences of satisfying them or continuing them dissatisfied on output should be conducted.
- **Simplicity in Motivational System:** The system should be simple both in terms of its understanding by the employees and its applicability in the organisation. Employees' efforts are directed to goal only when they perceive that a particular goal exists and this requires a particular type of effort. The system should be simple to be adopted by the organisation at various levels.
- **Uneven Motivation:** In an organisation, all the employees

are not of same type. They differ in education, attitude, ambition, etc. Thus, more educated and ambitious persons can be motivated up to a very high level, while others cannot be. If such employees are motivated beyond a certain limit, this may create frustration in them of being overloaded or unachievable goals creating frustration.

13.11 Morale

The satisfaction or dissatisfaction from the job results in psychological problem of morale. Morale is an individual's group feeling of competence and confidence reinforced by job satisfaction and need fulfilment. It may precede or follow performance and productivity. Morale is a total attitude towards one's work and one's colleagues. In work situations, it is a product of need satisfaction and job satisfaction level.

Different definitions of morale can be divided into three main categories:

- **Classical Approach:** The definition of Robert M. Guion can be put in this category. According to him, "Morale is defined as the extent to which individual needs are satisfied and the extent to which the individual perceives that satisfaction stemming from total job satisfaction".
- **Psychological Approach:** According to Filppo, Breach, Webstor and Nitles, etc., morale is psychological concept. According to them, morale is a state of mind and emotions affecting willingness to work which in turn affects individual and organisational objectives. Thus, it is a mental attitude of the individual which enables him to realise that the maximum satisfaction of his drives coincides with the fulfilment of the objectives of the company.
- **Social Approach:** Some modern writers describe morale as a social process. This concept is based upon Howthorne's experiments. The definitions of Prof. Elton Mayo, Keith Davis, Blankenship, Cohen and Moarse and Dale Yoder can be put in this category. According to Keith

Davis, "Morale can be defined as the attitudes of individuals and group towards their work, environment and towards voluntary cooperation to the full extent of their ability in the best interest of the organisation". Similarly, to quote Leighton, "Morale is the capacity of a group of people to pull together persistently and consistently in pursuit of a common purpose".

Thus, we see that on one hand, morale is a personal matter, while on the other hand, it is a group problem. As a matter of fact, it is an inner impulse explaining the attitude of a member employee towards his work, working conditions, fellow workers, management, job satisfaction and total organisation etc. It may be low or high. A high morale is reflected in zest, active cooperation, satisfaction, and appreciation, etc. While the indicators of low morale are passive cooperation, feeling of job as unimportant, work being a burden, hostility and apathy. According to T. Harell, "High morale is a spirit of whole hearted cooperation in a common effort".

13.12 Importance of Morale

Morale, productivity of workers and their level of motivation are directly correlated. As we know, motivation is an intrinsic ability and desire for positive efforts towards performance. The word motivation is derived from motive which is defined as an inner state that activates a man to do some work or channelise his behaviour towards goals. Hence, it is clear that if the level of morale is high, the motivation degree will also be high. If both these are high, the quantity of work done and the level of performance would also be high. Conversely, positive efforts and sound performance of job will also lead to high morale and motivation.

Thus, we can say that the level of morale of an efficient and capable worker will be high; simultaneously, he will be highly motivated too. But research studies have been unable to establish a conclusive and consistent correlation between motivation and morale. Sometimes, it happens that the morale is high but productivity is low or vice-versa. Similarly in some cases, high morale and low motivation may also co-exist. It is also possible to witness situations in which people suffering from low morale, nevertheless perform the assigned tasks rather well. But theoretically, we may say that motivation, productivity and morale go together.

The importance of morale can be illustrated with the statement of T. Harel who opined that 'high morale' is a confident spirit of whole hearted cooperation in a common effort. The statement of Dale Yoder also throws some light on the importance of morale in the following words:

"High morale is associated with the best motivation and success while low morale is the indicator of disappointment, enthusiasmlessness and loss of objectivity".

Keith Davis has compared morale to a lady when he writes, "Never underestimate the power of a woman. Simultaneously, do not underestimate the power of morale".

13.13 Factors Contributing to High Morale

There are various factors which contribute to high morale among workers of an industrial organisation. The management of the various enterprises use these factors in building the morale of their workers. Morale building is a continuous activity which means improving and maintaining the high level of morale among employees. It is a perpetual task and needs continuous efforts. C.E. Gregory has named it as the producer of climbing a moving ladder. Just as a moving ladder has no end of steps so also the process of morale building does not end. It implies that morale building is a continuous and complex process.

The steps of morale building can be divided into two groups: individual and group efforts. In this context, the group efforts are more practical, economical and effective. Hence, the managements generally try group efforts. Another way of classifying morale building efforts is to divide them as physical and psychological factors. Their detailed description is as follows.

13.13.1 Physical Factors for High Morale

A. Conditions of Work: The conditions of work have an important influence upon it. If the conditions of work favour the workers and create interest in the work, morale is likely to be high. On the contrary, if the conditions of work are not favourable and serve to distract the interests of the worker, morale is likely to fall. Conditions of work being a comprehensive term, it includes both physical and mental or psychological conditions. Various researches have led the belief that physical conditions of work have an important influence upon morale in the workers. As Tindall and Cair have proved on the basis of their experimentation, good conditions of work help to maintain a high morale. In this connection, Cair has pointed out the influence of music on the mental conditions of workers. Culier's experiments, seen to indicate that in bad conditions of work, morale tends to fall because the worker evinces signs of worry, distaste, irritability, anxiety, sleeplessness, laziness, lethargy, etc.

B. Position of Promotion: While studying the morale of various individuals in various positions of different companies, Arbrock came to the conclusion that the attitude of foremen is better than that of clerks while that of clerks is more favourable than is the case with other classes of workers. This study reveals that the morale of individuals is also susceptible to such influences as the post that he is holding. The main psychological fact at the root of this phenomenon is that if the individual in question does not get a position that concurs with his psychological bent of mind, his enthusiasm is lost and he loses confidence in those who are in authority above him. Hence, if morale is to be kept high in any and every industry, it is essential that posts be allotted in accordance with the ability and labour of the individuals, and that these posts be improved upon from time to time.

C. Increase in Salary: It is a psychological fact that workers are primarily concerned with their salary or wages. Shepard has stressed the fact that if the workers wages are reassessed from time to time and appropriate changes are made, the morale tends to occupy a high level. On the contrary, if the wages remain stationary for a long time, and there is no enhancement, the worker's enthusiasm is dampened, and they tend to heap blame on their officers. Increase in pay should be made dependent upon hard work or other qualities.

If increase in pay depends upon the personal idiosyncrasy of the individual in power, most people become cynical as they do not like to cringe before such a person. Secondly, even the ingratiating types who win increases in pay and promotions through subservience rarely have a high morale. Hence, for pay increase to have a favourable influence upon morale it is essential that the basis of increase be proper, and is the same for everyone.

D. Distribution of Salaries: Morale is also influenced by the method of distribution of salary. All studies to date on the subject have not led to any conclusive idea as to which method is definitely the best. Some methods are, of course, better than certain others.

E. Opportunity to Share Profit: Among the physical requirements, another one is the possibility and opportunity of progress in any concern. If the workers in a company are being paid dividends out of its profits, then it should be equally distributed. In other words, all workers should be given the opportunity to earn higher wages, without any discrimination.

If this is not done, most of them tend to turn against the authorities in their company while at the same time a feeling of jealousy for those who have progressed is engendered in the unfortunate ones. This destroys not only the collective organisational and administrative efficiency, but also faith and belief in the authorities. Hence, the rules governing promotion and increases in salary should be equally applicable to all, and they should be clearly understood by all of them. No one should be given a chance to complain on these grounds.

13.13.2 Psychological Factors:

A. Praise: It is a matter of general psychological knowledge that praise of good work and effort helps to infuse further enthusiasm and energy in a worker.

Studies conducted by such eminent psychologists like Thorndike and Harlock, evinced that praise of a worker's effort helps to increase his motivation. In fact, the influence of the reward and punishment scheme of work is fairly evident and widely known. Any work that derives punishment for the perpetrator is shunned by him in future, while he desires to repeat any work that results in reward. Praise is a psychological reward. Praise by individuals for whom we have respect and in whose judgement we have faith, matters a lot to us. If the authorities in the factory or office praise all good efforts, then morale becomes high among the workers. On the other hand, if good work and hard labour goes unnoticed, enthusiasm wanes in the worker, as he feels that he is not being valued according to his merits. This fact is one of the important reasons why work in an impersonal psychological organisation like government office is rarely of a high order of efficiency. Direct praise or blame is rarely forthcoming, except from some very conscientious individuals in authority.

B. Knowledge of Success: Some other experiments have brought to light the fact that if the worker is aware of the degree of success he is achieving in his work, his interest and enthusiasm in it are maintained, and so also the high level of morale. In very big factories where an individual work does no more than making only a very small cog in a very big wheel, and is not aware of the effect of his own effort towards the completed wheel, boredom, and disinterest is likely to set in very early. What is implied here is not the knowledge of the mere result. Result of work can be bad as well as good. Knowledge and failure can only serve to lower the morale, but if the worker is again encouraged to think in terms of success, morale can be regained. As a general rule, success ensures a high morale. Success is the reward of effort. And reward is a favourable element in the creation and maintenance of morale.

C. Fulfilment of Collective Needs: Man works not only to meet the needs of his body like food and clothing, but also to satisfy certain other collective psychological requirements. He is also desirous of meeting others, giving vent of his feelings and emotions, thoughts and beliefs, exhibiting himself, knowing himself, and winning social prestige and recognition. Any kind of work that affords all these advantages to the worker is almost certain to create a very high morale in him, but if all these things are not made available to him, morale is likely to fall, if it was ever high. Hence, in maintaining the morale of their workers, the organisers and authorities should keep in mind the fact that the workers' collective needs be also fulfilled and satisfied.

D. Freedom of Worker: In any company or factory, if a worker loses his identity to the extent of being reduced to the level of a small cog in a huge wheel, he is dissatisfied with his work because it appears heavy and insipid to him. Hence, in order to maintain the worker's morale at a high level it is essential that he be given the maximum degree of freedom that his function and position allows. He should also not be prevented from meeting other fellow workers, in particular those individuals who are in authority. It helps in creating a more intimate and knowledgeable atmosphere, in which he can tell his problems to the proverbial daddy. But the given freedom does not imply that discipline should be done away with. Independence within the framework of laws is the most desirable state of affairs.

E. Sense of Unity, Identity and Equality: It has been pointed out earlier that collective or group organisation is indicative of high morale. Hence, it is essential that a sense of organisation and unity should circulate freely among the workers. Psychologists, among them May and Wright, concluded from their examinations and study that in order to maintain a high morale among workers in industries, it is essential that the workers have in themselves a feeling of being organised, united or equal. The worker should be able to identify themselves with their factory or office or organisation and think of its interests as if they were his own. If this is achieved, even the most difficult times can be successfully seen through by making a collective effort.

Increase in the feeling of unity and identity can be facilitated by many things such as a definite name of the company or organisation, a definite dress and a common badge.

Besides these, certain group objectives can be set up, the achievement of which involves organised and collective effort on the part of the workers exerting oneself among with many others, striving for the same objective and which serve to lessen tension, increase mutual goodwill and organisation. Workers should be made to realise that they are an important and responsible part of the industry. They should also be equipped with knowledge of the various aspect of the industry, so that they come to look upon it as their own industry.

F. Others Factors: Apart from the above mentioned physical and psychological determinants of morale, there are some other factors that influence it, for example, through his experiments and research. The research of Arbork has shown that the level of morale is higher in the case of women workers than in the case of male workers.

Actually, maintaining a very high level of morale requires careful attention to be paid to all aspects of the worker's personality and to all aspects of his work. Handling grievances at proper stage and in time, employee counselling, delegation of authority and introducing suggestion schemes are other factors which can be instrumental in improving the morale of employees.

13.14 Methods of Measuring Morale

The main methods of measuring morale are the following.

13.14.1 Common Worker's Opinion Analysis: One very popularly used method of measuring the morale is the common worker's opinion analysis method in which the opinions of the average worker are collected and analysed. For this, certain scientific questionnaires are prepared that reveal the workers' opinions regarding various aspects of the industry as well as towards the authorities. The worker does not have to reveal his name in answering these questionnaires. This has the initial advantage of assuring the worker of secrecy regarding his views. When the questionnaires are received back after having been filled and duly completed by the workers, it becomes possible to see the various points on which the workers have complained. If some particular object or subject is a matter of complaint in a large majority of cases, efforts should be made to rectify it. Success in this method depends upon the degree to which the questionnaire is scientific, and upon the degree of truth in the workers' responses.

13.14.2 Interview Method: In this method, the individuals are directly interviewed who have departed from the unit in question, for various reasons. One main advantage of this method is that it reveals the reasons whereby the workers feel compelled to seek jobs elsewhere, so that future desertion on the part of present employees can be discouraged. Another feature of this method is that having left the employment of a particular concern or unit, one feels free to give expression to his frankest view on any and every aspect of the business. Another advantage of this method is that the views of departed employees cannot result in any harm to the administration or to those in authority.

There can be no doubt that some workers may have grievances against the administration regarding their job that has no relation whatsoever with actual and real conditions. But if many workers leave their jobs on the same pretext, than evidently, it is necessary to put an end to the source of complaint in order to maintain a high level of morale. In this manner, this method has proved extraordinarily useful in measuring the existing level of morale and suggesting methods of improvements. It also locates the cause of falling morale. If, however, most of the departed employees speak well and favourable of the work and the administration of the factory or business house, then there is very reason to believe that morale is at a high level.

13.14.3 Attitude Measurement: As has been pointed out earlier, morale is an expression of the feelings towards the work, the authorities and general administration in an organisation. Hence, the worker's attitudes can be known in order to evaluate their morale. For example, if the answer to the following queries were supplied by workers, their attitudes in these respects could be known.

- I work in the company under compulsion.
- The authorities in the company believe in the policy of paying as little wages as can practicably be paid.
- If I can get the same salary in a different company, I am prepared to resign from my present position.
- I have no respect for or faith in those in authority above me.
- The conditions of work in which I work cannot be said to be good by any standards.
- I find no freedom, pleasure or satisfaction in my work.

The workers' attitudes can be discovered by requiring them to mark the above queries right or wrong.

13.14.4 Sociological Methods: Nowadays, particularly in the case of group studies, the sociological methods are very prevalent. Moreover, a method for measuring the morale can be used to discover characteristics of the workers' group in an organisation whereby the level of morale can be discovered. In Jenken's experiment described earlier, only one aspect of the group organisation is included.

Accordingly, the worker is given a questionnaire containing certain questions intended to throw light on the characteristic of group organisation. For example, the workers are asked to name and enumerate the individuals with whom they would like to work, or under whom they would prefer to work, or in which sort of company do they prefer to spend their time or have anything to do with. If the answer of many individuals to this question seems to speak favourably for any one individual, and the answers seem to show respect, love and confidence for the individual, it is fairly evident that he is capable of becoming a good administrator. If he is already in the administrative cadre, then it evidences a high level of morale in the workers—for respect and confidence in authority is a sign of high morale.

But if he is not so situated, then the answer seems to show lack of confidence in the existing administration, a lack of confidence that can be rectified by promoting the desired individual into the administrative block, or otherwise by advising the existing administrative group to mend its ways and adopt other more calculated ways to win the confidence and respect of their subordinates. In this manner, it is evident that Moreno method can help in realising the condition of morale in any unit and in discovering the means of improving the existing morale.

13.14.5 Company Records and Reports: The records and reports of a company prepared for other reasons and purposes, can be used to measure the morale of the employees. These records can be analysed in the following manners: change of labour ratio, man-hour lost, absence and slackness, number of grievances reported by workers and resolved by the management, number and value of accidents that occurred in the factory, etc. These all variables can be interpreted as an index of morale.

13.15 Job Satisfaction

The importance of job satisfaction is fairly evident from a description of the importance of maintaining morale in any industry. If a worker is not satisfied with his work, then both the quantity and quality of his output will suffer. If his job satisfaction increases then there is an improvement in both the quality and quantity of production. Factories in which the workers are satisfied with their work are also characterised by a high morale. The following things are generally important for creating job satisfaction.

13.15.1 Attending and Solving Problems: It is desirable that the complaints of the workers he heard patiently and the problems solved as far as possible. Factories in which the worker's demands are not heeded to, suffer because the workers lose confidence in the management and become frustrated.

Every worker is definitely concerned about his future prospects. Factory rules clearly lay down the conditions of promotion and advancement, and if the worker gets the expected promotion and improvement in pay scales at the right time, he feels satisfied and becomes confident of the future. If on the other hand, the workers feel that even good work will not be rewarded, he becomes frustrated and slack in his work.

13.15.2 Testing the Workers' Ability and Progress: Every worker, whether in a factory or in office, desires that he should be paid according to his ability. If he has undergone some new training or has increased his ability to work in some way, he should be compensated for his better ability through a raise in salary. An organisation in which the management keeps an eye on the ability and progress of its worker, normally has a high degree of job satisfaction among their workers. It is necessary that the management should give the worker some opportunity of progressing higher and higher. If, on the other hand, the organisation does not pay any attention to the abilities and increased efficiency of its staff, it suffers in the long run because the worker also loses interest in his job and does not often try to improve his level of efficiency. This happens because they feel that an increase in qualifications or efficiency is not related to progress or promotion.

13.15.3 Respect for Creative Suggestions: Generally speaking, the worker working under a particular set of conditions is best qualified to say how and where improvements can be made. If workers are encouraged to suggest ways and means of improving the conditions of work, they often come with very valuable ideas. This helps in increasing job satisfaction because when the worker is praised for giving good practical ideas, he tends to pay more attention to his work in order to win more praise. If suggestions are neglected then the workers feel dissatisfied since apparently there can be no improvement in conditions in which he works.

13.15.4 Cordial Analysis or Evaluation of the Work: In every organisation, the manager or the supervisor has to offer criticism of the work performed by the worker because he must point out the worker's mistakes and try to eliminate them. If this criticism is offered in a cordial and friendly way, more as suggestion, his job satisfaction is also thereby enhanced. But if the worker is abused or bitterly criticised for his mistakes, he loses his peace of mind.

Rules governing increases in salary should be clear and explicit and should be acted upon impartially and regularly. If a worker gets the anticipated increase in salary at the right time, he feels satisfied with his job. If this does not happen, dissatisfaction is the result. Increase in salary is, in fact, the most important factor in job satisfaction.

If workers are not praised for exceptional performance in their work, they lose interest in it and as a result, the organisation suffers. Even if they do good work, they still remain dissatisfied and disgruntled. Generally, the worker prefers to work well and remain occupied than merely to pass the time allotted to him. If he is also encouraged in his work by an occasional word of praise and respect, he is further motivated to maintain a high level of efficiency and in fact to improve upon it. If he is not praised for his work, his enthusiasm and zeal falls immediately.

13.15.5 Promotion According to Ability: In every organisation, promotion is based upon the ability of the worker. If, on the other hand, promotion depends upon other factors such as casteism, personal favour, etc., than the workers' interest in his work declines.

If job satisfaction is to be maintained, it is essential that the quantity of work does not exceed the individual's ability to complete it. If he has to work more than he is comfortable with, the worker is bound to become disgusted, depressed and tired.

13.15.6 Satisfactory Hours of Work: The hours of work in any factory or offices should be convenient and so arranged so as to offer the least possible inconvenience to the maximum number of employees. If this is not looked into, the workers becomes dissatisfied.

References

References

Adler, N. (1997), "International Dimensions of Organizational Behaviour", 3rd edition, Cincinnatti, Ohio: South-Western.

Andrews, K.R. (1969), "Towards Professionalisation in Business Management".

Armstrong, M. (1977), "Principles and Practice of Personnel Management", Kogan, Page Ltd., London.

Bartlett, C. and Ghoshal, S. (1992), "Transnational Management: Text, Cases and Readings in Cross-border Management", Boston: Irwin.

Becker, B. and Gerhart, B. (1996), "The Impact of Human Resource Management on Organizational Performance: Progress and Prospects", *Academy of Management Journal*, 39(4): 779-801.

Berry, J.W. (1980), "Introduction to Methodology", in H.C. Triandis and J.W. Berry (eds.), Handbook of Cross-cultural Psychology, Volume 2, 1-28, Boston: Allyn and Bacon.

Bhagat, R.S. and McQuaid, S.J. (1982), "Role of Subjective Culture in Organizations: A Review and Directions for Future Research", *Journal of Applied Psychology,* 67: 653-685.

Brech, E.F.L. (1965), "Principles and Practice of Management", Longmans, Green and Co., London.

Brewster, C. and Hegewisch, A. (1994), "Policy and Practice in European Human Resource Management", Price Waterhouse Cranfield Survey. London: Routledge.

Caligiuri, P.M. and Stroh, L.K. (1995), "Multinational Corporate Management Strategies and International Human Resource Practices: Bringing IHRM to the Bottomline", *International Journal of Human Resource Management*, 6: 494-507.

Casico, W.F. (1989), "Managing Human Resources", McGraw-Hill, New York.

Cavusgil, S.T. (1993), "Internationalizing Business Education: Meeting the Challenge", East Lansing, MI: Michigan State University Press.

Chopra, R.K. (1969), "Management of Human Resources", V.K, Publishing House, Bareilly.

Cloude, S. George Jr. (1974), "The History of Management Thought", Prentice Hall of India, New Delhi.

Dale, D. Mc Conlsey (1967), "How to Manage by Results", AMA, New York.

Davar, Rustams (1988), "Personnel Management and Industrial Relations", Vikas Publishing House, New Delhi.

Dayal, L. and Adhibari, K. (1969), "Organisation and Administration", Progressive Corporation, Bombay.

Dessler, Gary (1999), "Human Resource Management", Prentice-Hall, New Delhi.

Druelser, Peter F. (1974), "Management: Tasks, Responsibilities and Practices", William Heinemann Ltd., London.

Elton, Maya (1953), "The Human Problems of an Industrial Civilization".

Feldman, D.C. (1988), "Management Career in Organisation", Scott, Foresman, Gleanview.

Flippo, Edwin B. (1981), "Principles of Personnel Management", McGraw-Hill, Tokyo.

Flippo, Edwin B. (1989), "Personnel Management", McGraw-Hill, New York.

French, Wendell, (1974), "The Personal Management Process", Houghton Mifflin and Co., Boston.

Gupta, Rakesh (1998), "Organisational Behaviour", Kitab Mahal, Allahabad.

Hall, Douglas T. (1976), "Careers in Organisation", Goodyear Publishing Co., Palisades, CA.

IIPM (1973), "Personal Management in India", Asia Publishing House, Bombay.

Kapoor, T.N. (1968), "Personnel Management and Industrial Relations in India", N.M. Tripathi (P) Ltd., Bombay.

Kimbal, D.S. and D.S. Kimbal Jr. (1971), "Principal of Industrial Organisation", Valsils Pfeffer and Simons, Bombay.

Mathur, J.S. and Mittal, S.K. (1989), "Personnel Management", Kitab Mahal, Allahabad.

Miner, J.B. and M.G. Miner (1977), "Personnel Management and Industrial Relations", Macmillan, New York.

Mooney, James D. (1947), "The Principles of Organization", Harper and Brothers, New York.

Patterson, S.H. (1943), "Social Aspects of Industry", Oxford University Press, London.

Paul, E. Torgesen and Irwin T. Weinstock, "Management: An Integrated Approach".

Phatak, A. (1997), "International Management: Concept and Cases", Cincinnati, Ohio: South-Western.

Phatak, A.V. (1995), "International Dimensions of Management", 4th edition, Cincinnati: South-Western.

Porter, M.E. (1985), "Competitive Advantage: Creating and Sustaining Superior Performance", New York: The Free Press.

Porter, M.E. (1986), "Changing Patterns of International Competition", *California Management Review,* 28(2): 9-40.

Prasad, Lallon (1973), "Personnel Management and Industrial Relations in Public Sector", Progressive Corporation, Bombay.

Pucik, V. (1997), "Human Resources in the Future: An Obstacle or a Champion of Globalization"? *Human Resource Management,* 36: 163-167.

Ricks, D.A. (1993), "Blunders in International Business", Cambridge, MA: Blackwell.

Schuler, R.S., Dowling, P.J. and De Cieri, H. (1993), "An Integrative Framework of Strategic International Human Resource Management", *Journal of Management,* 19: 419-459.

Schuler, R.S. and MacMillan, I.C. (1984), "Gaining Competitive Advantage through Human Resource Management Practices", *Human Resource Management,* 23(3): 241-255.

Scott, W.D., Clothier, R.C. and Sprirgel, W.R. (1986), "Personnel Management", Tata McGraw Hill, New Delhi.

Sibula, Andraw F. (1977), "Personnel Administration and Human Resource Management", John Wiley and Sons, New York.

Singh, B.P., Chhabra T.N.S. and Taneja, P.L. (1990), "Personnel Management and Industrial Relations", Dhanpat Rai and Sons, Delhi.

Sparrow, S., Schuler, R.S. and Jackson, S.E. (1994), "Convergence or Divergence: Human Resource Practices and Policies for Competitive Advantage Worldwide", *International Journal of Human Resource Management*, 5(2): 267-299.

Tayeb, M. (1994), "Organizations and National Culture: Methodology Considered", *Organization Studies,* 15(3): 429-446.

Taylor, S., Beechler, S. and Napier, N. (1996), "Towards an Integrative Model of Strategic International Human Resource Management", *Academy of Management Review*, 21: 959-985.

Teagarden, M.B. and VonGlinow, M.A. (1997), "Human Resource Management in Cross-cultural Contexts", *Management*

International Review, 37(1): 7-20

Theo, Haimann, "Professional Management", Eurasia Publishing House, New Delhi.

Yoder, Dale (1976), "Personnel Management and Industrial Relations", Prentice-Hall, New Delhi.

Index

Index